ScottForesman ENGLISH
On Your Mark 2

ROBERT D. LEE
Pasadena City College
Pasadena, California

DARLEEN A. LENNAN
Commonwealth of the Northern Mariana Islands
Public School System
Saipan

JACQUELINE L. LOVELACE
Dallas Independent School District
Dallas, Texas

MAYRA L. MENÉNDEZ, ED.S.
The School Board of Broward County
Florida

ScottForesman

A Division of HarperCollinsPublishers

I would like to thank my friends, colleagues, and family, especially my wife and children. Thanks Janice, Jennifer, and Stephen for your patience and understanding during my long and often late hours while this book was being written; you are troopers! I would also like to thank the staff at ScottForesman, especially Gloria Johnson, who shepherded us all.

Robert D. Lee

Thanks to Mimi Priestley and Patrick Lennan, whose lives are given to the education of children around the world; to Gloria Johnson and Mary Jane Maples, who worked tirelessly with the authors to make their ideas a reality; to Marcia Roebuck Hayden, who hired me; to my sons John and Gorden Videen, who have devoted the major parts of their careers to education; and to my parents, who constantly love and support me.

Darleen A. Lennan

I would like to thank my family, friends, and colleagues who gave me their support throughout the duration of this project. A special thank you goes to my three wonderful children, Rodney, Jr.; Leah; and Meagan, for their patience and understanding. Similarly, thanks are due to the excellent staff at ScottForesman for their treasured guidance. I also want to thank A.B. for the unfailing encouragement, advice, and support that I received.

Jacqueline L. Lovelace

To my parents, Emma and Ramón, and my sister, Neida, for all their encouragement and support throughout the years. Special thanks to Jack Shean, from ScottForesman for his confidence in my ability to undertake this endeavor. My appreciation to the staff at ScottForesman for all their patience, support, and assistance.

Mayra L. Menéndez, Ed.S.

CONSULTING REVIEWERS

Andrés A. Alonso, *Samuel L. Berliner School*
Newark, New Jersey

Joyce L. Butler, *Lantana Middle Community School*
Lantana, Florida

Sandra L. Cruz, *Hollywood High School, Los Angeles Unified School District*
Hollywood, California

Adriana López de Richards M.Ed, M.A., *Universidad Metropolitana de Ciencias de la Educación*
Santiago, Chile

Olga Lopez, *Newark Board of Education/Office of Bilingual Education*
Newark, New Jersey

Juana I. Marin-Arreje, *Escuelas Oficiales de Idiomas*
Madrid, Spain

Manuel J. Medina, *Chicago Public Schools/Chicago City Colleges*
Chicago, Illinois

Mary Sieu, Ph.D., *ABC Unified School District*
Cerritos, California

Lic. Deyanira Solis Juarez, *Language Center of the Normal Superior de Nuevo León*
Monterrey, Mexico

Christine Kay Williams, *Towson State University*
Baltimore, Maryland

Nancy Wilson-Webb, *Fort Worth Independent School District*
Fort Worth, Texas

We wish to thank the following people for their assistance in preparing these materials.

Carol Lethaby, *Instituto Tecnológico y de Estudios Superiores de Monterrey*
Guadalajara, Mexico

Mireya Morales de Patiño, *Instituto Iberoamericano de Idiomas*
CD. Victoria, Mexico

Acknowledgments will be found on page 132.

ISBN: 0-673-19593-7

Copyright © 1995

Scott, Foresman and Company, Glenview, Illinois.
All Rights Reserved. Printed in the United States of America.

This publication is protected by Copyright and permission should be obtained from the publisher prior to any prohibited reproduction, storage in a retrieval system, or transmission in any form or by any means, electronic, mechanical, photocopying, recording, or otherwise. For information regarding permission, write: Scott, Foresman and Company, 1900 East Lake Avenue, Glenview, Illinois 60025.

1 2 3 4 5 6 7 8 9 10 PRO 02 01 00 99 98 97 96 95 94

CONTENTS

A. Introductions

EXERCISE 1: *Introduce yourself to another student.*

A: Hi, I'm _____ . What's your name?

B: _____ .

A: What's your last name?

B: _____ .

A: Nice to meet you, _____ .

EXERCISE 2: *Now introduce your classmate to another student.*

A: Hi, _____ .

B: Hi, _____ .

A: _____ , this is _____ . **He's/She's** from _____ .

B: Hi, _____ . Nice to meet you.

C: Nice to meet you.

B. What to Say

 EXERCISE 3: *Ask your classmates these questions.*

1. Where are you from?
2. Where do you live?
3. How old are you?

C. Months

EXERCISE 4: *Read the questions. Mark your answers on the calendar.*

1. When's your birthday? Circle the month.
2. When's your friend's birthday? Find the month. Write an *X*.
3. What months are you in school? Write an *S* in each month.

D. Forms

NEW STUDENT INFORMATION FORM

Name: _Yakamoto_ _Kenji_
 Last First

Address: _3557 West 12th Street_

Phone Number: _(212) 555-5892_

Age: _16_ **Birthday:** _October 9_

Native Country: _Japan_

 EXERCISE 5: *Answer the questions about Kenji's form.*

1. What's his first name?
2. Where does he live?
3. What's his phone number?
4. When's his birthday?
5. Where's he from?

 EXERCISE 6: *Fill out the form with information about yourself.*

NEW STUDENT INFORMATION FORM

Name: _____
 Last First

Address: _____

Phone Number: _____

Age: _____ **Birthday:** _____

Native Country: _____

WARM UP

EXERCISE 1: *Answer the questions.*

1. When is Junko's birthday?
2. When is Alma's birthday?
3. When is your birthday?
4. Do Junko and Alma have different birthday celebrations?

Please give your homework to me on Tuesday. Remember, there's no school on Monday because it's a holiday. It's Martin Luther King, Jr. Day.

But Monday is January 19th. I know that Martin Luther King, Jr.'s birthday is January 15th.

Martin Luther King, Jr.

In the United States, we celebrate some holidays on Monday so we can have a long weekend.

That's a good idea.

V VOCABULARY

Holidays

Some U.S. Holidays	
Martin Luther King, Jr. Day	third Monday in January
Presidents' Day	third Monday in February
Mother's Day	second Sunday in May
Memorial Day	last Monday in May
Father's Day	third Sunday in June
Labor Day	first Monday in September
Thanksgiving	fourth Thursday in November

 EXERCISE 2: *Ask and answer questions about the chart above.*

A: When is Martin Luther King, Jr. Day?
B: It's on the third Monday in January.

MAY

	SUN	MON	TUE	WED	THU	FRI	SAT
first week	1 Be Kind to Animals Week	2	3	4 School Librarian Day	Children's Day in Japan, Teacher Day, Cinco de Mayo **5**	6	7
second week	**8** Mother's Day	9	10	11	12	13	14
third week	15	16	17	**18** International Museum Day	19	20	21
fourth week	22	23	24	African Freedom Day, Argentine Independence Day **25**	26	27	28
fifth week	29	**30** Memorial Day	31				

School Librarian Day is always on May 4.
Children's Day in Japan is always on May 5.
Teacher Day and Cinco de Mayo are always on May 5 too.
Mother's Day is always on the second Sunday in May.
International Museum Day is always on May 18.
African Freedom Day is always on May 25.
Memorial Day is always on the last Monday in May.

EXERCISE 3: *Ask and answer questions about the calendar on page 6.*

A: When is Teacher Day?
B: It's always on May 5.

EXERCISE 4: *Write the word or words under the picture.*

cake	candles	friends	presents
calendar	decorations	ice cream	

1. _____

2. _____

3. _____

4. _____

5. _____

6. _____

7. _____

WORD FOR WORD

A. Ordinal Numbers in Dates

1st	first	11th	eleventh	21st	twenty-first
2nd	second	12th	twelfth	22nd	twenty-second
3rd	third	13th	thirteenth	23rd	twenty-third
4th	fourth	14th	fourteenth	24th	twenty-fourth
5th	fifth	15th	fifteenth	25th	twenty-fifth
6th	sixth	16th	sixteenth	26th	twenty-sixth
7th	seventh	17th	seventeenth	27th	twenty-seventh
8th	eighth	18th	eighteenth	28th	twenty-eighth
9th	ninth	19th	nineteenth	29th	twenty-ninth
10th	tenth	20th	twentieth	30th	thirtieth

EXERCISE 5: *Work with a partner. Look at the calendar for February. Take turns asking and answering questions. Use ordinal numbers.*

A: When's Groundhog Day?
B: February second.
B: When's Junko's birthday?
A: February seventh.

Michael Jordon

Edward J. Olmos

Yoko Ono

FEBRUARY

SUN	MON	TUE	WED	THU	FRI	SAT
		1	2 Groundhog Day	3	4	5
6	7 *Junko's Birthday*	8	9	10	11	12 Lincoln's Birthday
13	14 Valentine's Day	15	16	17 Michael Jordan's Birthday	18 Yoko Ono's Birthday	19 Presidents' Day
20	21	22 Washington's Birthday	23	24 Edward J. Olmos's Birthday	25	26
27 Dominican Republic Independence Day	28		**Black History Month**			

B. In/On

> In the U.S., Mother's Day is always **in May**.
> This year, Mother's Day is **on May 9**.
> Mother's Day is always **on Sunday**.

MAY

SUN	MON	TUE	WED	THU	FRI	SAT
2	3	4	5	6	7	1
Mother's Day 9	10	11	12	13	14	8
16	17	18	19	20	21	15
23/30	24/31	25	26	27	28	29

EXERCISE 6: *Look at the calendars and read about these holidays in the U.S. Write __in__ or __on__ and the correct month, date, or day.*

JUNE

SUN	MON	TUE	WED	THU	FRI	SAT
		1	2	3	4	5
6	7	8	9	10	11	12
13	14	15	16	17	18	19
20 Father's Day	21	22	23	24	25	26
27	28	29	30			

1. We celebrate Father's Day _in_ June.

2. Father's Day is always _on_ Sunday.

3. Father's Day is _on_ June 20 this year.

OCTOBER

SUN	MON	TUE	WED	THU	FRI	SAT
				1	2	3
4	5	6	7	8	9	10
11	12	13	14	15	16	17
18	19	20	21	22	23	24
25	26	27	28	29	30	31 Halloween UNICEF Day

4. Halloween and UNICEF Day are _in_ October.

5. They're always _on_ October 31.

6. Halloween and UNICEF DAY are _____ Saturday this year.

NOVEMBER

SUN	MON	TUE	WED	THU	FRI	SAT
1	2	3	4	5	6	7
8	9	10	11	12	13	14
15	16	17	18	19	20	21
22	23	24	25	26 Thanksgiving	27	28
29	30	31				

7. We always celebrate Thanksgiving _____ the fourth Thursday _____ November.

8. This year, Thanksgiving is _____ November 26.

EXERCISE 7: *Tell a partner about a holiday in your native country. Tell the month and the date. Tell the day of the week if you know it. Use __in__ or __on__.*

G GRAMMAR

A. Frequency Words

> We **always** stay home from school on Martin Luther King Day.
>
> Do you **usually** go to school on Groundhog Day?
>
> Yes, but we **never** go to school on Saturday or Sunday.
>
> ---
>
> Does your teacher **often** tell you about holidays?
>
> Yes, he does. He **sometimes** celebrates holidays with us too.

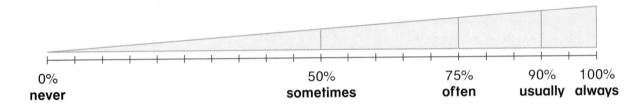

| 0% | | | | | | 50% | | | 75% | | 90% | 100% |
| never | | | | | | sometimes | | | often | | usually | always |

EXERCISE 8: *Write the correct words. The % tells you the frequency word to use.*

We [0%] _never have_ school on January 1

     have/has

because it's New Year's Day.

1. I [90%] _____ to bed late on December 31.

    go/goes

2. We (50%) _____ to a fireworks show on July 4.

    go/goes

3. I (75%) _____ candy on Valentine's Day.

    get/gets

4. I (100%) _____ a party on my birthday.

    have/has

5. The groundhog (75%) _____ its shadow on

    see/sees

February 2.

6. We (0%) _____ pizza for Thanksgiving dinner.

    have/has

EXERCISE 9: *Tell a partner about what you do on certain holidays. Use* <u>usually</u>, <u>often</u>, *or* <u>sometimes</u>. *Take turns.*

A: On Chinese New Year's Day, I **often** wear new clothes.

B: On Mother's Day, I **sometimes** give my mother flowers.

B. There is/There are

There is a holiday in May.	
Is there a holiday in September?	Yes, **there is.**
Is there a holiday this Monday?	No, **there isn't.**
	No, **there's not.**
There are thirty days in June.	
Are there thirty days in September?	Yes, **there are.**
Are there thirty days in February?	No, **there aren't.**

EXERCISE 10: *Does anyone in your class have a birthday in March? If so, write the name or names on the calendar below. Then write* <u>Is there</u> *or* <u>Are there</u> *on the lines.*

MARCH

SUN	MON	TUE	WED	THU	FRI	SAT
		1	**2**	**3** Jackie Joyner Kersee's Birthday	**4**	**5**
6 Michelangelo, born 1475	**7**	**8**	**9**	**10**	**11**	**12**
13	**14**	**15**	**16**	**17** St. Patrick's Day	**18**	**19**
20	**21**	**22**	**23**	**24** Greek Independence Day	**25**	**26**
27	**28**	**29**	**30**	**31**		

_____*Is there*_____ a famous artist's birthday in March?

1. _____ thirty days in March?

2. _____ a school holiday in March?

3. _____ a famous athlete's birthday in March?

4. _____ an Independence Day in March?

5. _____ any March birthdays in this class?

Jackie Joyner Kersee

EXERCISE 11: *Look at the calendar for March. Ask and answer the questions you wrote in Exercise 10.*

A: Is there a famous artist's birthday in March?

B: Yes, there is. Michelangelo's birthday is on March 6.

LISTENING

 EXERCISE 12: *Listen. Circle the date.*

March 3   March 13   (March 23)

1. June 7   June 17   June 27

2. October 3   April 3   August 3

3. June 14   July 4   January 4

4. February 17   February 27   February 7

5. February 4   February 14   February 24

6. September 7   September 17   September 2

7. November 22   November 12   November 27

 SPEAKING

EXERCISE 13: *Ask your partner the questions. Take turns.*

EXERCISE 14: *Tell about your partner's answers to Exercise 13.*

(Partner's name) birthday is on _____ .

He/She usually _____ on his/her birthday.

His/Her favorite holiday is _____ .

On (holiday) , **he/she** _____ .

 **READING**

Read Laura's letter to Sofia.

Laura Hansen
3506 Harlem Ave.
Chicago, IL 60634
U.S.A.

Sofia Spinelli
34, via Garibaldi
Rome, ITALY

Dear Sofia,

January 18

Hi! How are you?

I don't have school tomorrow because tomorrow is Martin Luther King, Jr. Day. When I have a day off, I usually get up at nine o'clock. Then I go to my friend Carmen's house or Carmen comes to visit me. We often play video games. Sometimes, we go to the park and play basketball. Sometimes, we go to the shopping mall.

What do you usually do when you have a day off from school? Do you go shopping with your friends? Do you go to the park?

I hope that you can visit me some day or that I can visit you. It would be fun to meet you and your family.

Your friend,
Laura

 EXERCISE 15: *Complete the list about Laura.*

	What does Laura usually do on a school holiday?
1.	
2.	
3.	
4.	
5.	

WRITING

  EXERCISE 16: *Complete the list about yourself.*

	What do you usually do on a school holiday?
1.	
2.	
3.	
4.	
5.	

EXERCISE 17: *Write a letter to a friend. Tell what you do on a school holiday. Use your list in Exercise 16. Use <u>always</u>, <u>usually</u>, <u>often</u>, or <u>sometimes.</u>*

Dear _____ ,

_____

_____

_____

_____

_____

_____

_____

_____

_____ ,

_____

WARM UP

TODAY'S MENU

chicken	$1.09	carrots	$.29	rice	$.29	banana	$.25
fish	$1.09	potatoes	$.29	bread	$.19	apple	$.25
				orange juice	$.29		
				milk	$.29		

1.

2. Can I help you, Anita?

Yes, I'd like some chicken and rice.

3. Would you like a vegetable?

The carrots look good. I'll have some carrots.

4. Would you like some fruit?

Yes, please. I'd like a banana.

5. Anything to drink?

I'll have a glass of orange juice.

6. Chicken and rice, carrots, banana, and orange juice. That'll be $2.21.

Here's $3.00.

7. OK. Seventy-nine cents is your change.

Thank you.

 EXERCISE 1: *Answer the questions.*

1. What is Anita having for lunch?
2. How much does it cost?
3. What would you like for lunch?
4. How much does it cost?

V VOCABULARY

A. What would you like?

EXERCISE 2: **Work with two partners. Take turns ordering the different kinds of food in the picture.**

A: What would you like?

B: I'd like an egg and an orange, please.

A: That'll be fifty cents.

A: What would you like?

B: I'd like some potatoes, two eggs, and a tomato, please.

A: That'll be $1.18.

B. That looks delicious!

 EXERCISE 3: *Write the correct word under the picture.*

apple	bread	egg	orange	potato
bananas	carrots	fish	grapes	tomato

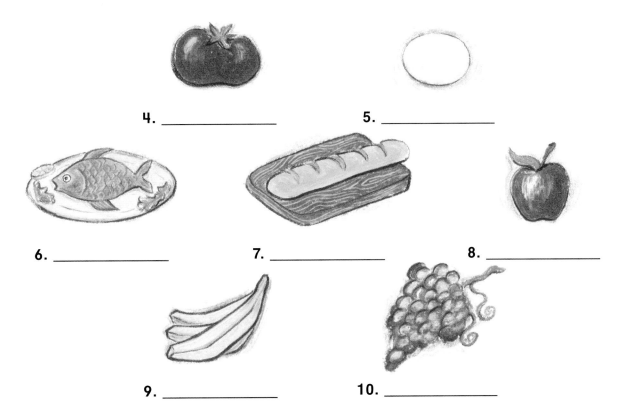

1. _____

2. _____

3. _____

4. _____

5. _____

6. _____

7. _____

8. _____

9. _____

10. _____

WORD FOR WORD

Amounts of Food

I'd like **a cup** of soup, please.
a bowl of soup
a loaf of bread
a carton of milk
a bottle of juice
a glass of water
two slices of pizza
a bag of grapes
a can of beans
two pieces of cake
two boxes of cereal

EXERCISE 4: *Ask and answer questions about food. Use the words in dark type and the pictures to answer.*

two cans

A: What would you like?
B: I'd like two cans of orange juice, please.

1. **a loaf**
2. **a box**
3. **two glasses**
4. **a piece**
5. **a carton**
6. **a bag**
7. **two cups**
8. **two bottles**
9. **two slices**
10. **two bowls**

G GRAMMAR

A. Count/Noncount Nouns

How many apples do you want? **How many potatoes** do you want?	One, please. Two, please.
How much beef do you want? **How much soup** do you want?	Two slices, please. A cup, please.

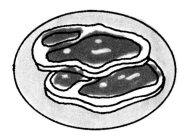

EXERCISE 5: *Write the words from the list in the correct boxes.*

bananas	cheese	fish	rice
bread	chicken	oranges	sandwiches
carrots	eggs	potatoes	tomatoes

How many _____ do you want?	How much _____ do you want?
bananas	*bread*

EXERCISE 7: *Look at the menu on page 15. Ask questions with How much or How many.*

A: How much chicken would you like?

B: Two pieces, please.

B. *Linking Verbs:* Look, Taste, Smell

> The fish **looks** good.
> These grapes **taste** delicious.
> This milk **smells** awful.

EXERCISE 8: *Complete each sentence with a word from Column 1 and a word from Column 2.*

<u>Column 1</u>
looks/look
smells/smell
tastes/taste

<u>Column 2</u>
awful
delicious
good

The soup ___*smells good*___ .

1. This apple *taste delicious* .

2. The orange _____ .

3. This pizza *smells good* .

4. This egg _____ .

5. These tomatoes _____ .

6. The carrots _____ .

LISTENING

 EXERCISE 9: *Finish David's grocery list. Write the amounts you hear.*

Shopping List

Milk   —   1 carton _____

1. bananas — _____

2. oranges — _____

3. beans   — _____

4. rice   — _____

5. bread   — _____

SPEAKING

EXERCISE 10: *Work with a partner. You work at the cafeteria. Your partner wants to order some food. Use the menu on page 15. Take turns.*

Can I help you?

Yes, I'd like _____ , _____ , _____ , and _____ .

That'll be $_____ .

Here's $_____ .

OK. $_____ is your change.

EXERCISE 11: *Tell about your partner's food order in Exercise 10.*

(Partner's name) wants _____ , _____ , _____ , and _____ .

_____ pays $_____ .

_____ gets $_____ in change.

 **READING**

The Food Guide Pyramid shows the foods we need to eat every day.
Read about how many servings from each food group we need to eat.

**FOOD GUIDE
PYRAMID**

Fats, Oils, and Sweets
USE SPARINGLY

Milk, Yogurt,
and Cheese
Group
2-3 SERVINGS

Meat, Poultry, Fish,
Dry Beans, Eggs
and Nuts Group
2-3 SERVINGS

Vegetable
Group
3-5 SERVINGS

Fruit
Group
2-4 SERVINGS

Bread, Cereal,
Rice, and Pasta
Group
6-11 SERVINGS

Source: U.S. Department of Agriculture/U.S. Department of Health and Human Services

EXERCISE 12: *Read about Anita. Answer the question. Write the food groups on the lines.*

Anita had chicken and rice, a serving of carrots, a banana, and a glass of milk for lunch. From which food groups did she eat?

chicken *the meat, poultry, fish, dry beans, eggs, and nuts group*

1. rice _____

2. carrots _____

3. banana _____

4. milk _____

EXERCISE 13: *On a sheet of paper, write down everything you eat for one day. Then use the list to fill in the chart below.*

EXERCISE 14: *Complete the chart with the foods you listed in Exercise 13. Write how many servings of each food group you had. Then look at the numbers of servings The Food Guide Pyramid says you need. Do you have the same numbers?*

Pyramid Food Group	My Servings
1. milk, yogurt, and cheese	
2. vegetable	
3. bread, cereal, rice, and pasta	
4. fruit	
5. meat, poultry, fish, dry beans, eggs, and nuts	
6. fats, oils, and sweets	

WRITING

EXERCISE 15: *Teresa's health class is learning about food groups. Teresa wrote about her favorite lunch. Read what Teresa wrote. Then tell a partner about your favorite lunch.*

My favorite lunch is a slice of ground beef and cheese pizza, an apple, a piece of carrot cake, and milk. The food groups in my favorite lunch are:

pizza: bread, cereal, rice, and pasta
     milk, yogurt, and cheese
     vegetable
     meat, poultry, fish, dry beans, eggs, and nuts
     fats, oils, and sweets
apple: fruit

carrot cake: vegetable
           bread, cereal, rice,
           and pasta
           fats, oils, and sweets
milk: milk, yogurt, and cheese

EXERCISE 16: *On a sheet of paper, write about your favorite lunch.*

UNIT 3 Morning, Noon, and Night

WARM UP

1. **Do you usually watch "The Late Show" on TV, Marc?**

   No, I can't stay up late on week nights because I have to get up early in the morning.

2. **What time do you get up?**

   Six o'clock.

3. **Why so early?**

   Well, before I leave for school, I have to take a shower, get dressed, have breakfast, and brush my teeth. I have to leave for school by 7:20 so I can get to my first class at eight.

4. **That's early! My first class is at 8:30. I live only three blocks from school, so I don't have to leave until 8:15.**

   You're lucky, Carlos!

EXERCISE 1: *Answer the questions.*

1. Why can't Marc stay up late on week nights?
2. How much time does Marc have between the time he gets up and the time he leaves for school?
3. Why doesn't Carlos have to leave for school until 8:15?
4. How much time do you have between the time you get up and the time you leave for school?

VOCABULARY

A. Breakfast, lunch, and dinner

1. It's 7:30 in the morning. Lucy is having breakfast. Today she is having a glass of orange juice, some eggs, and some bread.

2. It's noon. Lucy is having lunch in the school cafeteria. Today she is having a chicken sandwich, a salad, an apple, and some orange juice.

3. It's 4:00 in the afternoon. Lucy is having a snack. Today she is having a banana and some milk.

4. It's 6:30 in the evening. Lucy is having dinner at home with her family. They're having fish, rice, carrots, and salad.

 EXERCISE 2: *Ask and answer questions about when you have breakfast, lunch, dinner, and a snack.*

A: What time do you usually have breakfast?

B: I usually have breakfast at 7:15.

B. What are your routines?

1. Andrew gets up early in the morning.

2. Then he takes a shower.

3. After he takes a shower, he gets dressed.

4. Then he combs his hair.

5. After he has breakfast, he brushes his teeth.

6. Then he goes to school.

7. After he gets home from school, he does his homework.

8. He has dinner early in the evening.

9. Before he goes to bed, he watches TV.

10. He goes to bed late at night.

 EXERCISE 3: *Ask and answer questions about your routines in the morning, afternoon, and evening.*

A: What do you do in the morning?

B: I get up at 7:00. Then I _____ .

EXERCISE 4: *The sentences are about Paulette's daily routine. Match each sentence to its picture. Write the letter on the line.*

a. Paulette gets up.
b. She takes a shower.
c. She gets dressed.

d. She combs her hair.
e. She has breakfast.
f. She brushes her teeth.

g. She has a snack.
h. She has dinner.
i. She goes to bed.

1. _____

2. _____

3. _____

4. _____

5. _____

6. _____

7. _____

8. _____

9. _____

WORD FOR WORD

A. Times of Day

I study	in the morning. in the afternoon. in the evening.	I see my friends	at noon. at night.
		I go to bed	at midnight. at (ten) o'clock.
		I have a snack	at 3:00 in the afternoon.

EXERCISE 5: *Complete the sentences with <u>in</u> or <u>at</u>.*

I have a lot of things to do **(1)** _____ the morning. After I get up, I brush my teeth. I take a

shower and get dressed. After breakfast, I go to school. Classes start **(2)** _____ 8:00. I have

lunch **(3)** _____ noon. After school, I usually have a snack. I try to do all my homework

(4) _____ the afternoon. My family eats dinner together. Sometimes I watch TV **(5)** _____

the evening. I usually go to bed **(6)** _____ 10:00.

EXERCISE 6: *Work with a partner. Take turns asking and answering questions about*
yourselves.

in the evening

A: What do you usually do in the evening?
B: On weekday evenings, I usually have dinner and do my homework.
  On weekend evenings, I usually have dinner and watch TV.

1. at noon
2. in the afternoon
3. in the morning
4. at 3:00 in the afternoon
5. at night

B. Go/Go to/Go to the

After school, I **go** home.
　　　　　　　　downtown.

In the morning, Tim **goes to** school.
　　　　　　　　　　　　class.
　　　　　　　　　　　　band practice.

We **go to the** library every afternoon.
　　　　　　　shopping mall
　　　　　　　park
　　　　　　　post office

EXERCISE 7: *Complete the sentences with a form of* <u>go</u>, <u>go</u> <u>to</u>, *or* <u>go</u> <u>to</u> <u>the</u>.

On weekdays, Carmen and I are very busy. In the morning, we **(1)** _go to the_ school. After school, Carmen **(2)** _goes to_ downtown. She **(3)** _goes to_ library downtown because she has a part-time job there. She sometimes **(4)** _goes to_ post office to mail letters.

On Tuesdays and Thursdays, I **(5)** _go_ soccer practice after school, but on the other days, I **(6)** _go_ home. I usually do homework, but sometimes I **(7)** _go_ supermarket with my mother. We always buy a lot of food there. Then we **(8)** _go to the_ home.

EXERCISE 8: *Today is Friday. Look at the ads. Work with a partner. Talk about where you want to go tomorrow.*

A: What do you want to do tomorrow?
B: We can go to the museum. It opens at 9:00 in the morning.

▪▪▪▪ ENTERTAINMENT HIGHLIGHTS ▪▪▪▪

The Mystery in the Everglades
Cinema Theater
2:15, 4:15, 6:15, 8:15

Tigers vs. Hawks
at Central Stadium
Tonight at 7:00 PM

The True Story of the Dinosaurs
Natural History Museum
museum hours: 9:00 AM to 5:00 PM

Multicultural Art Show
at Jackson Park
Saturday at 8:00 AM to 5:00 PM

G GRAMMAR

A. Before/After

| I eat breakfast at 7:30 in the morning.
I go to school at 8:00 in the morning. | **Before** I go to school, I eat breakfast.
After I eat breakfast, I go to school. |

EXERCISE 9: *The clocks and the words show Jenny's routine. What does she do first?*
Make sentences with your partner. Use <u>before</u> and the correct verb forms.

Before she combs her hair, she gets dressed.

1.
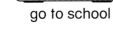

    take shower   get dressed

2.

    go to school   eat breakfast

3.

    go home   go to her locker

EXERCISE 10: *These clocks and words show Mark's routine. What does he do last?*
Make sentences with your partner. Use <u>after</u> and the correct verb forms.

After he has lunch, he goes to math class.

1.

    brush his teeth   have breakfast

2.

    get to school   go to his locker

3.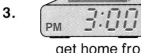

    get home from   eat a snack
    school

EXERCISE 11: *Tell a partner about your routine. Use the words below. Take turns.*

before have breakfast
Before I have breakfast, I get dressed.

1. **after** have breakfast
2. **before** go to school
3. **after** get out of school
4. **after** have dinner
5. **before** go to bed

B. Have to/Has to

Do you and Sue **have to go** home now?	No, we **don't**. We **don't have to go** home until 8:00.
Does Jason **have to do** his homework now?	Yes, he **does.**
What **do** you **have to do** today?	I **have to go** to the dentist.
What **does** Lin **have to do** today?	She **has to go** to the drugstore.

EXERCISE 12: *Look at the pictures. What does Juan have to do? Tell your partner. Take turns.*

Juan has to get up at 7:00.

EXERCISE 13: *Work with a partner. Ask and answer this question.*

A: What do you have to do today?

B: _____

LISTENING

EXERCISE 14: *Listen to Elena's conversation with Judy. Read the sentences.*
*Circle **T** for true and **F** for false.*

1. Elena is going to the basketball game.   **T   F**

2. Elena has to get up at 6:30.   **T   F**

3. Elena has band practice at 7:30.   **T   F**

4. Before Elena gets dressed, she walks her dog.   **T   F**

5. Elena has a big breakfast.   **T   F**

6. Judy has a big breakfast too.   **T   F**

 SPEAKING

EXERCISE 15: *Ask your partner the questions. Take turns. Fill in the box with your*
partner's answers.

Before School	After School

EXERCISE 16: *Tell about your partner's answers to Exercise 15.*

Before school, _____ . Then _____ .

After school, _____ . Then _____ .

READING

Read about Alma's activities before school and after school.

My name is Alma. I have a lot to do tomorrow before I go to school.
I have to get up at 7:00. After I take a shower, I have to comb
and dry my hair. After breakfast, I have to brush my teeth. Then I
have to take a bus to get to school by 8:30.

After I get out of school at 3:30, I have to take a bus to the library.
I have to get some books there. I have to be home by 5:30 to help my
brother make dinner. We eat at 6:30. Then I have to wash the dishes.
Then I have to finish my homework. At 10:00 I have to brush my teeth and go to bed.

EXERCISE 17: *List Alma's activities in her schedule book. Write the time of the
activity if it is in the paragraphs above.*

Name: *Alma Estrada*	Day: *Tuesday*
Before School: *7:00 A.M. Get up*	
After School:	

WRITING

EXERCISE 18: *Write your schedule for tomorrow in the chart.*

Name:	Day:
Before School:	
After School:	

EXERCISE 19: *Write two paragraphs about your schedule on a sheet of paper.*

WARM UP

EXERCISE 1: *Answer the questions.*

1. Where is Marc going?
2. What does he need?   *Mineeds to go to the*
3. Where is Chen going?
4. What does Marc want?
5. Why can't Marc give Chen any money?

 EXERCISE 2: *Answer the questions.*

1. Where is Cristina going?
2. What does she want to do there?
3. What does Emily want to do?
4. What kind of store does the boy need to find?
5. How can he get to the store?

V VOCABULARY

A. Can I help you?

EXERCISE 3: *Choose items in the picture to buy. Ask and answer questions about them.*

A: Can I help you?

B: Yes. I'd like to buy this compact disc and these two magazines.

A: OK. That'll be $17.95.

B. Where do they need to go?

 EXERCISE 4: *Work with a partner. Read each need that Sam or Carmen has. Take turns saying where he or she needs to go.*

Sam doesn't have any bread or fruit.
He needs to go to the grocery store.

1. Sam wants to rent a video.
2. Sam's car is out of gas.
3. Sam wants to buy toothpaste and a comb.
4. Carmen wants to buy a CD for her friend.
5. Carmen has to take a bus.
6. Carmen wants to shop for jeans and a shirt.

brush   magazine   toothbrush
comb   newspaper   toothpaste
compact disc   tape   video
gas

1. _____

2. _____

3. _____

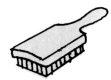

4. _____

5. _____

6. _____

7. _____

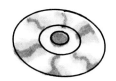

8. _____

9. _____

10. _____

EXERCISE 6: **Work with a partner. Ask and answer questions. Use the cues and the map.**

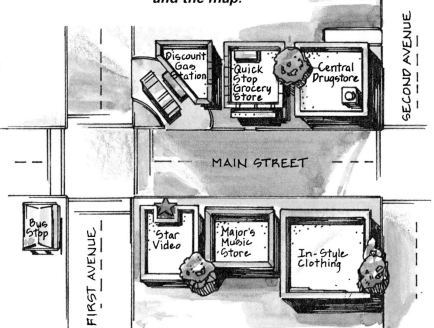

video

A: Where can I get a video?
B: You can get one at Star Video.
A: Where's Star Video?
B: It's on the corner of Main Street and First Avenue.

1. toothbrush
2. T–shirt
3. gas
4. magazine
5. fruit
6. CD
7. newspaper

UNIT 4   SHOPPING IN MY NEIGHBORHOOD

WORD FOR WORD

I want to buy **this**.	I want to buy **that**.
I want to buy **this** CD.	I want to buy **that** newspaper.
I want to buy **these**.	I want to buy **those**.
I want to buy **these** tapes.	I want to buy **those** magazines.

EXERCISE 7: *Complete the sentences with* <u>this</u>, <u>these</u>, <u>that</u>, *or* <u>those</u>.

I want to buy *that* newspaper.

Does _____ bus go to the park?

1.

Please take _____ bags to my car.

2.

I want to buy _____ shoes.

3.

I want to rent a video from _____ store.

4.

I want to read _____ book.

5.

40   **UNIT 4   SHOPPING IN MY NEIGHBORHOOD**

GRAMMAR

A. Questions with Verb + Infinitive

Where **does** Ruben **want to go?** Why **does** he **want to go** there?	He **wants to go** to the music store. Because he **needs to buy** a tape.
Do you **want to rent** a video? **Does** Mei **need to go** to the bank?	Yes, I **want to rent** "Jurassic Park." No, she **doesn't need to go** there.

EXERCISE 8: *Work with a partner. Use the cues to make questions to ask your partner. Take turns asking and answering.*

Where / want / go for lunch?

A: Where **do** you **want to go** for lunch?
B: I want to go to Hamburger House.

1. Where / need / go after this class?
2. What / want / do after school today?
3. Do / need / do any homework for tomorrow?
4. Do / want / go to the shopping mall on Saturday?
5. What / want / buy?

EXERCISE 9: *Read the answer. Write the question.*

Do you want to go to the movies?

No, I don't want to go to the movies.

Where does he want to go?

He wants to go to a seafood restaurant.

1. _Do you need a toothbrush_

Yes, she needs to get a toothbrush.

2. _____

I want to go to Jan's Clothing Store.

3. _____

I want to go there because I need to buy a new sweater.

4. _____

No, he doesn't want to go the video store.

B. Simple Present Tense vs. Present Progressive Tense

What **are** you doing now?	I'**m making** dinner.
Where **is** Tara going?	She'**s going** to the bank.
Are you **making** pizza?	Yes, I **am**.

The simple present tense tells what happens a lot and how people feel.
We usually use <u>like</u>, <u>need</u>, and <u>want</u> in the simple present tense.

What **do** you **do** on Monday nights?	I **go** to band practice.
What **does** Rex **want** for dinner?	He **wants** a pizza.
Do you **like** carrots?	No, I **don't**.

EXERCISE 10: *Read sentences from Olga's letter. Circle the correct verb form.*

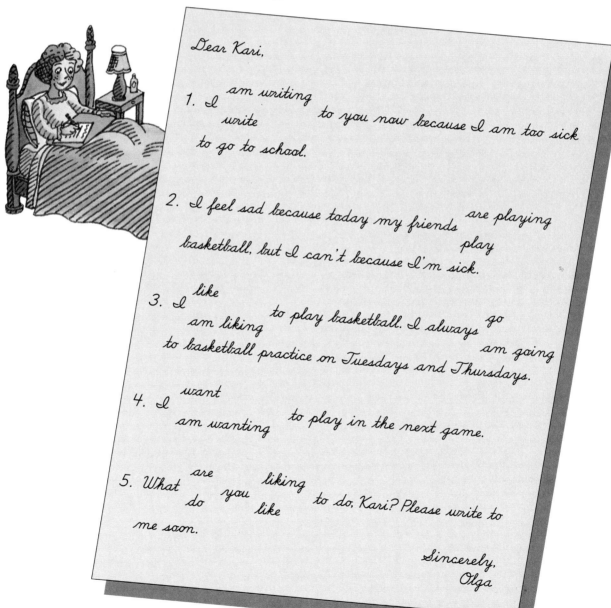

Dear Kari,

1. I $\begin{array}{c}\text{am writing}\\\text{write}\end{array}$ to you now because I am too sick to go to school.

2. I feel sad because today my friends $\begin{array}{c}\text{are playing}\\\text{play}\end{array}$ basketball, but I can't because I'm sick.

3. I $\begin{array}{c}\text{like}\\\text{am liking}\end{array}$ to play basketball. I always $\begin{array}{c}\text{go}\\\text{am going}\end{array}$ to basketball practice on Tuesdays and Thursdays.

4. I $\begin{array}{c}\text{want}\\\text{am wanting}\end{array}$ to play in the next game.

5. What $\begin{array}{c}\text{are}\\\text{do}\end{array}$ you $\begin{array}{c}\text{liking}\\\text{like}\end{array}$ to do, Kari? Please write to me soon.

Sincerely,
Olga

LISTENING

  EXERCISE 11: *Listen to each conversation. Circle the correct words.*

Conversation 1

1. The woman needs to buy a   **magazine**   newspaper.
2. She needs to go to   **Better Grocery**   **Better Drugstore.**
3. It's on   **Fourth Avenue**   **Main Street.**

Conversation 2

1. The man wants to buy a   **tape**   **CD.**
2. He needs to go to   **Central Drugstore**   **Mac's Music.**
3. It's on   **Main Street**   **High Street.**

Conversation 3

1. The woman wants to buy a   **T-shirt**   **sweater.**
2. She needs to go to   **The Clothes Closet**   **the music store.**
3. The store is   **in the shopping mall**   **on High Street.**

 SPEAKING

 EXERCISE 12: *Ask your partner the questions. Take turns.*

Where do you like to shop for clothes?

Where do you buy food?

Where can you rent videos in your neighborhood?

Where do you usually wait for the bus?

EXERCISE 13: *Tell about your partner's answers to Exercise 12.*

(Partner's Name) likes to shop for clothes at _____.
_____ buy / buys food at _____.
_____ can rent videos at _____.
_____ waits for the bus _____.

READING

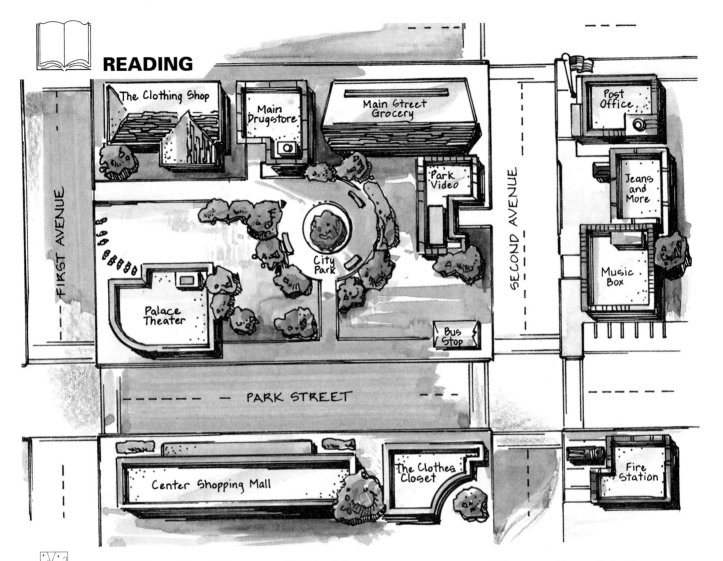

 EXERCISE 14: *Read the map. Work with a partner to answer the questions. Take turns.*

1. What's the name of the music store?

2. Where's the bus stop?

3. Where can you buy toothpaste?

4. Where's the movie theater?

5. What's next to the music store?

6. Where can you go to buy milk?

WRITING

EXERCISE 15: *Where do you get things in your neighborhood? Read the paragraph that Angela wrote about her neighborhood. Then, on a sheet of paper, write about your neighborhood and draw a map that shows the places you described.*

My name is Angela. I can do a lot of things in my neighborhood. I can rent videos at Park Video. I can mail letters at the Post Office. I can buy jeans at a clothing store called Jeans and More. I can get tapes and CDs at the Music Box. My favorite place in the neighborhood is the Palace Theater. My family and I like to see new movies there.

WARM UP

EXERCISE 1: *Answer the questions.*

1. What does Seng see out the window?
2. What does Maypa do to help?
3. What does the emergency operator ask Maypa?
4. What will happen next?

EXERCISE 2: *Ask and answer questions.*

1. What happened to María?
2. Who calls 911?
3. What information does the operator ask for?
4. Where are Janet and her friend?

VOCABULARY

A. Fire! Police!

1. My car is on fire!

2. Our garage is on fire!

3. Our neighbor's house is on fire!

4. Someone stole my wallet!

5. Someone stole my purse!

6. A burglar broke into our apartment!

 EXERCISE 3: *Act out making calls about all of the emergencies in the pictures.*

A: 911. Emergency.
B: Help! My car is on fire!
A: Where are you?
B: On Cherry Street, next to Jim's Supermarket.
A: A fire truck will be there soon.

A: Police Department.
B: Someone stole my wallet!
A: Where are you now?
B: At home. 436 North Broadway.
A: OK. A police officer will be there in an hour.

B. Call an ambulance!

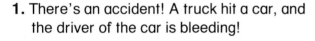

1. There's an accident! A truck hit a car, and the driver of the car is bleeding!

2. She's unconscious! She's hardly breathing!

3. He can't breathe! He's choking on something!

4. She fell off her bike! I think she broke her leg!

 EXERCISE 4: *Work with a partner. Act out making calls about all of the emergencies in the pictures. Tell what happened. Take turns.*

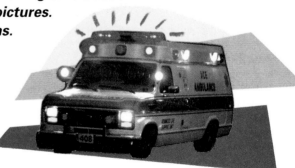

A: 911. Emergency.
B: Help! I just saw an accident. A truck hit a car, and the driver of the car is bleeding!
A: Where's the accident?
B: On Interstate 94 East near the Lake Street exit.
A: OK. An ambulance will be there soon.

---

accident   ambulance   burglar   car   emergency   purse   truck   wallet

1. My _____car_____ is on fire!

2. A _____burglar_____ broke into our house.

3. Someone stole my _____wallet_____ .

4. Help! This is an _____ .
My house is on fire!

5. We saw an _____accident_____ .

6. The _____ went off the road.

7. Someone stole
my mother's _____purse_____ .

8. The _____ is on its way now!

WORD FOR WORD

Two-Word Verbs

> A burglar **broke into** a store and took some money.
> The burglar **ran into** me.
> I **fell down** and hurt my knee.
> When I **got up,** I didn't have my wallet.
> I think the burglar **picked up** my purse and **took out** my wallet.

EXERCISE 6: *Complete the conversations. Write the correct words on the lines.*

fell down   ran into   took out   get up   pick up   broke into

1. A: Did you _____ my books?

   B: No, I only have my own books.

2. A: What did the burglar take from your book bag?

   B: He _____ all of my books.

3. A: Ouch!

   B: What happened?

   A: I _____ the table.

4. A: I can't _____. I think I broke my leg.

   B: I'll call 911.

5. A: What happened to your apartment?

   B: A burglar _____ it and stole my TV.

6. A: How did you hurt your knee?

   B: I _____ the stairs.

GRAMMAR

A. The Simple Past Tense

Regular Verbs	
The Simple Present Tense	**The Simple Past Tense**
I always **call** 911 in an emergency. Accidents sometimes **happen** here·	Yesterday, I **called** 911. This morning an accident **happened** on our street.

Irregular Verbs	
The Simple Present Tense	**The Simple Past Tense**
I sometimes **break** things. Marta sometimes **falls** down. We sometimes **see** accidents. Trucks sometimes **hit** cars. Ben sometimes **takes** the bus. Burglars often **steal** things. Jenny **runs** every morning. I usually **get** groceries on Thursdays. We usually **go** to Rob's Grocery.	I **broke** a window yesterday. She **fell** down last night. We **saw** a car accident yesterday. A truck **hit** a car this morning. Ben **took** the bus yesterday. A burglar **stole** our TV set last night. This morning she **ran** for half an hour. This week, I **got** groceries on Friday. On Friday, we **went** to Best Grocery.

EXERCISE 7: Complete the paragraphs. Write the past-tense form of each verb.

I (**1. see**) _____saw_____ an accident yesterday. It (**2. happen**)_____ on the corner of Lake Street and Fifth Avenue. A truck (**3. hit**)_____ a bus. No one (**4. get**) _____ hurt.

Hillel (**5. run**) _____ to the bus stop because he was late. He (**6. fall**) _____ as he was getting on the bus and (**7. break**) _____ his leg. The bus driver (**8. call**) _____ 911.

A burglar (**9. steal**) _____ our CD player last week. We think he (**10. get**) _____ in and (**11. go**) _____ out through the window. He didn't know our CD player was broken!

B. The Simple Past Tense: Information Questions

What did you **see?**	I **saw** an accident. A blue car **hit** a green car.
Where did it **happen?**	It **happened** in front of my school.
When did it **happen?**	It **happened** at about 3 o'clock today.
How did it **happen?**	The green car **turned** left on a red light.

EXERCISE 8: *Write the correct form of each verb. Remember to use
<u>did</u> in past-tense questions.*

A: What (**1. do**) _____ you _____ last night?

B: I (**2. go**) _____ to the movies.

A: Who (**3. go**) _____ you _____ to the movies with?

B: I (**4. go**) _____ with my friend, Lori.

A: What movie (**5. see**) _____ you _____?

B: We (**6. see**) _____ "Emergencies."

A: How was it?

B: Great! In one accident scene, a car (**7. run**) _____ into a building.

A: Did the driver get hurt?

B: Yes. He (**8. break**) _____ his leg. An ambulance came and

(**9. take**) _____ him to the hospital.

A: Another scene in the movie was about a girl who (**10. fall**) _____ out of a tree.

B: Why was she in the tree?

A: It's a long story.

B: Sorry. I don't have time to hear it.

LISTENING

  EXERCISE 9: *Listen to the 911 calls. Circle the correct information about each call.*

Caller One

1. Peter is reporting   **an accident**   **a fire**   **a burglary.**

2. The person on the floor is   **choking**   **unconscious**   **bleeding.**

3. The   **police**   **fire truck**   **ambulance**   will be there right away.

Caller Two

1. Elsa called 911 to report a   **fire**   **accident**   **burglary.**

2. The neighbor's   **house**   **truck**   **garage**   is on fire.

3. The   **ambulance**   **police**   **fire truck**   will be there in 15 minutes.

Caller Three

1. Darren called the   **accident**   **ambulance**   **emergency**   number.

2. A burglar   **ran into**   **broke into**   **stole**   his home.

3. The   **fire truck**   **police**   **ambulance**   will be there in 30 minutes.

 # SPEAKING

 EXERCISE 10: *Ask your partner the questions. Take turns.*

> Did you ever have an accident? / Did you ever see an accident?

> What happened?

> How did it happen?

> When did it happen?

 **READING**

South Park Police Department Accident Report

Date: March 12 **Time:** 11:45 A.M.	**Injuries:** Frank Forest's head was bleeding. An ambulance took him to Community Hospital. Elena Moreno did not need to go to the hospital.
Location: Columbus Drive and Fourth Avenue	
What happened? Frank Forest was on Columbus Drive. He went through a red light and hit Elena Moreno's car. Elena Moreno was on Fourth Avenue crossing Columbus Drive.	**Traffic ticket issued to:** Frank Forest
	Police officer: Felicia Ramirez

  EXERCISE 11: *Answer the questions about the accident report.*

1. When did the accident happen?
2. Where did the accident happen?
3. What happened?
4. Why did Frank Forest get a ticket?

 WRITING   **EXERCISE 12:** *You work in the emergency room at Community Hospital. Write about the accident in these pictures.*

Community Hospital Emergency Room Report

Patient's Name: Juana Cruz	**Date:** April 11 **Time:**
Location:	**Injuries:**
What happened?	
	Emergency room clerk's signature:

UNIT 6 School Activities

WARM UP

EXERCISE 1: *Answer the questions.*

1. Where did Scott go?
2. Did he like the dance?
3. Did Julio like the band?
4. Why didn't Julio see Scott?

___

 EXERCISE 2: *Answer the questions.*

1. When did the boys' volleyball team play their game?
2. Do you think they won the game? Why?
3. Who did Rita vote for to be student council president?
4. What does Rita want to do in the next election?

VOCABULARY

A. What did they do on Monday?

1. **Monday:** attended an assembly.

2. **Tuesday morning:** voted in an election.

3. **Tuesday evening:** went to a band concert.

4. **Wednesday morning:** attended a student council meeting.

5. **Wednesday afternoon:** went to a volleyball game.

6. **Thursday:** went to a science fair.

7. **Friday:** went to a dance.

EXERCISE 3: Ask and answer questions about all of the pictures.

A: What did they do on Monday?
B: They attended an assembly.

B. What did they do at school?

1. They decorated the gym.

2. They danced to the band.

3. They marched in the band.

4. They cheered for their team.

5. They ran for student council.

6. They voted in the school election.

7. She ran in the race.

8. He entered the science fair.

EXERCISE 4: *Ask and answer questions about all of the pictures.*

A: What did they do to the gym?
B: They decorated it.

assembly	band	election	science fair
auditorium	dance	game	student council

1. _____

2. _____

3. _____

4. _____

5. _____

6. _____

7. _____

8. _____

WORD FOR WORD

Object Pronouns

I	me	Lin went to the game with **me**.
you	you	Rosa and I looked for **you**.
he	him	I didn't vote for **him**.
she	her	I voted for **her**.
it	it	Ed saw your art work, but I didn't see **it**.
we	us	Please come to the next dance with **us**.
they	them	Meg and Al went to the dance. I saw **them**.

 EXERCISE 6: *Read. Write the correct object pronoun. Use each pronoun one time.*

My friend María wanted to go to the volleyball game on Friday, so I went to the game with **(1)** _____ . We saw María's brother at the game, so we sat with **(2)** _____ . We looked for you, but we didn't see **(3)** _____ .

Our team hit the ball a lot, but the other team didn't hit **(4)** _____ very much. We like the players on our team, so we cheered for **(5)** _____ .

Would you like to go to the next game with **(6)** _____ ? Maybe María can go with **(7)** _____ too.

EXERCISE 7 *Work with a partner. You are at a school dance. You are looking for your friends. Use the picture and the words to ask and answer questions. Use* <u>me</u>, <u>you</u>, <u>him</u>, <u>her</u>, <u>it</u>, <u>us</u>, *or* <u>them</u>.

Jack
A: Do you see Jack?
B: No, I don't see him.

Pedro
A: Do you see Pedro?
B: Yes, I see him.

1. Sonia
2. Junko and Tony
3. Dan and Luis
4. the food
5. the guitar player in the band

G GRAMMAR

A. The Simple Past Tense: Yes/No Questions

Did you **study** for your math test? **Did** you **talk** to Inés?	Yes, I **did**. No, I **didn't**.
Did Mayra **march** in the band? **Did** she **cook** dinner?	Yes, she **did**. No, she **didn't**.
Did all of the students **vote**? **Did** all of them **attend** the assembly?	No, they **didn't**. Yes, they **did**.

EXERCISE 8: *Work with a partner. Ask five questions with* <u>Did you</u>... *Answer with* <u>Yes,</u>
        <u>I did</u> *or* <u>No,</u> <u>I didn't</u>. *Take turns.*

A: Did you go to school yesterday?   A: Did you go to art class?
B: Yes, I did.   B: No, I didn't.

EXERCISE 9: *Read each question and answer. Write* <u>did</u> *or* <u>didn't</u> *and the correct words.*

attend	**go**	**study**	**vote**
cook	**march**	**talk**	

A: _____ Dimitri _____ to you last night?

B: Yes, he _____. He called me at seven o'clock.

1. A: _____ Elena _____ the assembly in the
auditorium?

   B: No, she _____. She went to the doctor's office.

2. A: _____ Jeff _____ dinner last night?

   B: Yes, he _____. He made pizza for everyone.

3. A: _____ Lourdes _____ for you?

   B: No, she _____. She voted for her boyfriend.

4. A: _____ Steve _____ to the volleyball game?

   B: No, he _____. He had to do his homework.

5. A: _____ Yolanda _____ for the history test?

   B: Yes, she _____. She studied for three hours.

B. The Simple Past Tense: Regular Verbs

I **cheered** for the team last night.
I **didn't cheer** for the team yesterday.

Ted **decorated** the gym yesterday.
He **didn't decorate** the gym today.

Sonia **danced** at the school dance last night.
She **didn't dance** at the school dance last month.

We **marched** in the band yesterday.
We **didn't march** in the band on Friday.

They **studied** for their English test last night.
They **didn't study** for their science test.

cheer + ed = cheered
study + ed = studied
stop + ed = stopped

EXERCISE 10: *Who did these activities? Who didn't do them? Work with a partner. Look at the pictures. Say what Pablo and Amy did and didn't do.*

Pablo

Amy

vote
Pablo voted yesterday.
Amy voted yesterday too.

play volleyball
Amy played volleyball yesterday.
Pablo didn't play volleyball yesterday.

1. march in the band
2. call someone on the phone
3. decorate the school gym
4. dance at the school dance

EXERCISE 11: *What did you do yesterday? What didn't you do? Tell a partner.*

A: I studied English, and I played soccer. I didn't study math. What about you?
B: I played in the band, and I went to PE class. I didn't go to art class.

 LISTENING

  EXERCISE 12: *Listen. What did Luz, Kim, Karen and Sam do? Write an X.*

	Luz	Sam	Karen	Kim
played in the band concert	X			
1. went to the football game				
2. went to the science fair				
3. studied for a test				
4. went to the dance				

 SPEAKING

 EXERCISE 13: *Ask your partner the questions. Take turns.*

What did you do at school last week?

(Ask more questions about your partner's activities.)

 EXERCISE 14: *Tell about your partner's answers to Exercise 14.*

READING

Read the school newspaper article.

DÍAZ IS NEW STUDENT COUNCIL PRESIDENT

The student council election was on September 16.

Here is how we voted. Ana Díaz won the election for president. She got 104 votes and Juan Gómez got 87 votes. John Kraus got 75 votes. For vice-president, Tuan Lee got 145 votes and won the election. Lucas Silva got 121 votes. Congratulations, Ana and Tuan!

Our secretary and treasurer are returning from last year. The secretary is Amina Chandar, and the treasurer is LaToya Miller. The first student council meeting is on October 2.

— • **●** • —

 EXERCISE 15: *Who won the election? How many votes did they get?*
Fill in the chart.

	Name	Votes
President:		
Vice-President:		

EXERCISE 16: *Answer the questions.*

1. When was the election?
2. Who are the four officers of the student council?

 WRITING

 EXERCISE 17: *Write notes for a newspaper article about an activity in your school.*

What happened? _____

When did it happen?_____

Where did it happen? _____

Who was there?_____

EXERCISE 18: *Use your notes in Exercise 17 to write your newspaper article on a sheet of paper.*

WARM UP

EXERCISE 1: *Answer the questions.*

1. Who is Max looking for?
2. What does she look like?
3. Point to her in the picture. What is she doing?
4. Where are Max and David?

EXERCISE 2: *Answer the questions.*

1. Who does Jenny call?
2. Where is Ana?
3. What does Jenny look like?
4. What does Elena look like?

VOCABULARY

A. Is he heavy or thin?

1. Eric is heavy.   **2.** Gerard is thin.   **3.** Mike is tall.   **4.** Cathy is short.

5. Lin has long hair.   **6.** Carla has short hair.   **7.** Joe has straight hair.   **8.** Dan has curly hair.

EXERCISE 3: *Ask and answer questions about all of the people in the pictures.*

A: Is Eric heavy or thin?
B: He's heavy.

EXERCISE 4: *What do you look like? Ask a partner. Take turns.*

1. Are you heavy or thin?
2. Are you tall or short?
3. Is your hair long or short?
4. Is your hair straight or curly?

B. What does he look like? What does she look like?

1. What does Peter look like?

He is tall and heavy.
He has short brown hair.
He has blue eyes.

2. What does Nancy look like?

She is of average height.
She has long blond hair.
Her hair is straight.
She has blue eyes.

3. What does Teresa look like?

She is of average height.
She has short black hair.
She wears glasses.

EXERCISE 5: *Look at the picture. Ask and answer questions about Kenji, Gary, and Fatima.*

A: Is Kenji tall?
B: No, he's short.
A: Does he wear glasses?
B: Yes, he does.

EXERCISE 6: *Look at the picture. Complete each sentence with the correct word.*

black	long
blond	short
brown	straight
curly	tall
glasses	thin
heavy	

1.   2.   3.   4.   5.   6. 7.   8.   9.

1. Sharon wears _____ so she can see clearly.

2. Joe is tall and a little_____.

3. Carmen is _____ and thin.

4. Kim has _____ brown hair. Her hair is _____.

5. Chen has short _____ hair. His hair is straight.

6. Al has straight _____ hair.

7. Samantha is tall and _____.

8. Crystal has curly _____ hair.

9. Robert is _____ and heavy.

WORD FOR WORD

Be/Have/Wear

I am short.	I have long hair.	I wear glasses.
Marcos **is tall.**	Mina **has brown eyes.**	My brother **wears glasses.**
My sisters **are thin.**	Peter and Al **have curly hair.**	My parents **don't wear glasses.**

EXERCISE 7: *Complete each sentence with the correct forms of* be*,* have*, and* wear*.*

I **(1)** _____ of average height, and I **(2)** _____ thin. I **(3)** _____

short brown hair. I **(4)** _____ blue eyes. I don't **(5)** _____ glasses.

My friend Rob **(6)** _____ short and heavy. He **(7)** _____ long brown hair. He

(8) _____ glasses. His parents **(9)** _____ glasses too. Rob and his parents all

(10) _____ brown eyes.

EXERCISE 8: *Describe yourself and other people to a partner. Use forms of* be*,* have*, and* wear *and the cues below. Take turns.*

1. I
2. My (brother / sister)
3. My (math) teacher
4. My friend

G GRAMMAR

Order of Adjectives

Sonia is a **tall, thin** girl.
She has **long, straight** hair.
She has **big blue** eyes.
She's wearing a **pretty red** sweater.
Mr. Hill is a **short, heavy** man.
He has **curly brown** hair.
He's wearing a **nice black** jacket.

EXERCISE 9: *Look at the adjectives in the box. Then circle the correct word to complete each sentence.*

1. Use **tall** or **short** before / after **thin** or **heavy**.

2. Use **long** or **short** before / after **straight** or **curly**.

3. Use **red** or another color word before / after another adjective.

EXERCISE 10: *Complete the sentences about the two people in the picture. Use two adjectives in the correct order in each sentence.*

1. Jack is a _____ _____ boy.

2. He has _____ _____ hair.

3. He's wearing a _____ _____ jacket.

4. Alicia is a _*tall*_ _*ku*_ girl.

5. She has _____ _____ hair.

6. She's wearing a _____ _____ jacket.

LISTENING

 EXERCISE 11: *Listen to the conversations. Write 1 under the person described in Conversation 1. Write 2 under the person described in Conversation 2. Write 3 under the person described in Conversation 3.*

 SPEAKING

 EXERCISE 12: *Work with a partner. Secretly choose a person from Exercise 11. Your partner asks you questions about that person. After you answer the questions, your partner can point to the person in the picture. Take turns.*

READING

Read these ads for pen pals.

• • • • PEN PAL ADS • • • • PEN PAL ADS • • • •

PEDRO RAMIREZ, 16, lives in Mexico. He has curly brown hair and brown eyes. He likes to play soccer and go to movies.

DILLON YEATS, 17, lives in Ireland. He has straight red hair and blue eyes. He likes to read, write, and hike.

DALIA SCHWARTZ, 16, lives in Israel. She has curly brown hair and brown eyes. She likes listening to music, dancing, and playing sports.

YOKO TANAKA, 16, lives in Japan. She likes going to restaurants, museums, and movies. She has straight black hair and brown eyes.

EXERCISE 13: *Work with a partner. Answer the questions.*

1. Where does Yoko live?
2. How old is Dillon?
3. What does Pedro look like?
4. What does Dalia like to do?

Michael Baker
745 Washington Street
Boston, MA 02215

BOSTON MA

Pedro Ramírez
Calle Mesones 44
Mexico City, MEXICO

Read this letter to a new pen pal.

745 Washington Street
Boston, MA 02215
September 5

Dear Pedro,

Hi! I'd like to be your new pen pal.

My name is Michael Baker. I live in Boston, Massachusetts. I am 16 years old, the same as you. I have straight brown hair and blue eyes. Like you, I like to play soccer. I also like to play baseball and listen to music.

Please write to me soon.

Sincerely,
Michael

EXERCISE 14: *Work with a partner. Answer the questions about the letter.*

1. Where does Michael live?
2. How old is Michael?
3. What does Michael look like?
4. What does Michael like to do?

WRITING

 EXERCISE 15: *Fill in the chart with information about yourself for a pen pal ad.*

Name	
Age	
Country	
Height	
Hair	
I like to...	

EXERCISE 16: *Write a pen pal ad about yourself. Use the information you wrote in Exercise 15 and the pen pal ads on page 73 as models.*

_____

_____

_____

EXERCISE 17: *Choose a pen pal from the ads on page 73. Write a letter to your new pen pal. Use the information in your ad in Exercise 16 to write about yourself.*

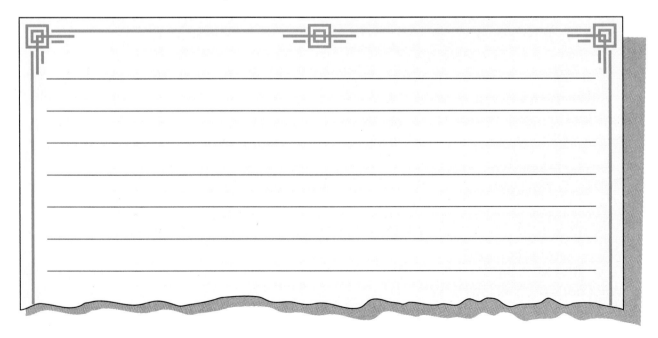

WARM UP

Welcome back! How was your vacation?

It was great! Thanks for asking.

Where did you go?

I visited my family in Mexico.

Did you go by plane?

Yes, we flew to Mexico City from Chicago.

How long did it take you to get there?

Four hours.

Wow! How long were you there?

Three weeks.

What did you do?

We went to the National Museum of Anthropology and the Palace of Fine Arts, and we saw the ballet in Mexico City. Then we went to Acapulco for one weekend. We liked the beach there.

It sounds like you had a fun vacation!

EXERCISE 1: *Answer the questions.*

1. Where did the boy go on vacation?
2. How long was he there?
3. How long did it take to fly to Mexico City from Chicago?
4. Where did he go for the weekend?
5. What kinds of things do you think he saw at the National Museum of Anthropology?

VOCABULARY

A. Where did he go on his vacation?

1. beach

2. ocean

3. mountains

4. museum

5. ballet

6. airport

7. hotel

EXERCISE 2: *Point to each picture. Ask and answer the questions.*

A: Where did he go on his vacation?
B: He went to the beach.

A: Where do you want to go on your vacation?
B: I want to go to the mountains.

B. Where is it?

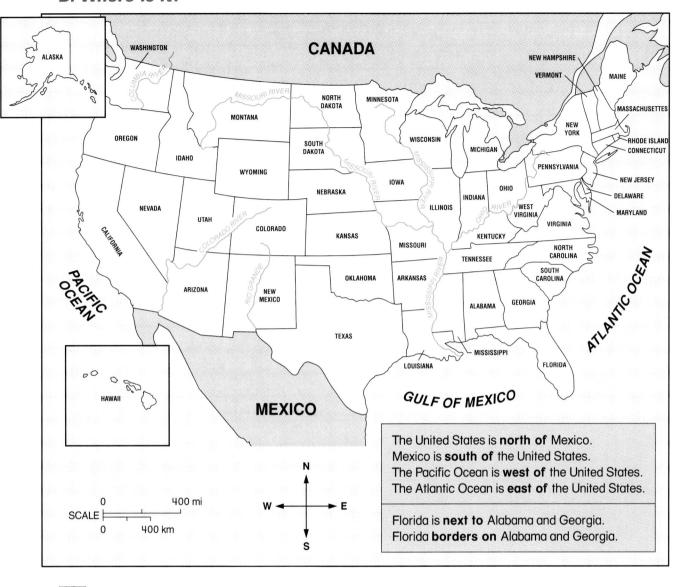

The United States is **north of** Mexico.
Mexico is **south of** the United States.
The Pacific Ocean is **west of** the United States.
The Atlantic Ocean is **east of** the United States.

Florida is **next to** Alabama and Georgia.
Florida **borders on** Alabama and Georgia.

EXERCISE 3: *Where is it? Use the words to ask and answer questions about places on the map.*

A: Where is Utah?
B: Utah is west of Colorado.

A: Where is Colorado?
B: It's north of Arizona.

1. Where is California?
2. What states are next to Mexico?
3. Where is North Carolina?
4. Where is Florida?
5. Where is Maine?
6. What states border on Kansas?
7. Name three states south of the Ohio River.
8. Name three states that border on the Pacific Ocean.

EXERCISE 4: *Write the correct word under the picture.*

airport   beach   mountains   ocean
ballet   hotel   museum

1. _____

2. _____

3. _____

4. _____

5. _____

6. _____

7. _____

WORD FOR WORD

Transportation

How did you get to Seattle?
I got to Seattle **by bus.**

by bike   **by train**   **by car**   **by plane**   **by motorcycle**

 EXERCISE 5: *Ask and answer the questions about the people in the pictures.*

A: How did Roberto get to school?
B: He got there by bike.

1. How did David get to New York City?

2. How did Mei get to California?

3. How did Michael get to Chicago?

4. How did Casey get to Washington, D.C.?

G GRAMMAR

A. The Simple Past Tense: To Be

uri	*eguy*
Where **were** you last week?	I **was** on vacation last week.
Where **was** Susan last week?	She **was** on vacation too.
How long **was** Greg on vacation?	He **was** on vacation for ten days.
How **was** your vacation?	It **was** fun!
Where **were** you and Nan yesterday?	We **were** at the park.
Where **were** Fred and Max yesterday?	They **were** at the soccer game.

EXERCISE 6: *Read. Write the correct word. Use* <u>was</u> *or* <u>were</u>.

Last week I **(1)** _____ on vacation with my family. We **(2)** _____ in Hawaii.

My mother and I **(3)** _____ there for one week. My father **(4)** _____ there for

two weeks. He went there early because he did some work there.

We liked Hawaii. The ocean **(5)** _____ beautiful. The water **(6)** _____ warm,

and the waves **(7)** _____ huge. The mountains **(8)** _____ beautiful too. Our hotel

(9) _____ close to lots of restaurants and to the beach.

EXERCISE 7: *Read. Complete each question and answer with* <u>was</u> *or* <u>were</u>.

1. A: Where _____ you last month?

   B: I _____ in Italy. I went there with my grandmother.

3. A: How long _____ you there?

   B: We _____ there for three weeks.

5. A: How _____ the food there?

   B: It _____ delicious!

2. A: _____ the pizza the same as the pizza in the U.S.?

   B: No, it _____ different, but I liked it.

4. A: _____ the people friendly?

   B: Yes. They _____ kind and helpful.

6. A: Why _____ you there?

   B: We _____ visiting my grandmother's friends.

EXERCISE 8: *Complete the questions with* <u>was</u> *or* <u>were</u>. *Then work with a partner. Ask and answer the questions.*

1. Where _____ you yesterday?
2. How long _____ you there?
3. How _____ it?

B. The Simple Past Tense: Yes/No Questions and Short Answers with To Be

Were you sick yesterday?	Yes, I **was.**
Were you at school?	No, I **wasn't.**
Was Sam at the game last night?	Yes, he **was.**
Were you and Rita at the theater?	Yes, we **were.**
Were Ted and Luis at the gym?	No, they **weren't.**

was + not = wasn't
were + not = weren't

EXERCISE 9: *Work with a partner. Ask a question with the word* <u>was</u> *or* <u>were</u>. *Use the map to answer questions about Kim and Tracy and Antonio.*

Kim and Tracy in San Diego

A: Were Kim and Tracy in San Diego?
B: Yes, they were.

1. Antonio in Los Angeles
2. Antonio in Palm Springs
3. Kim and Tracy in Fresno
4. Antonio in San Jose
5. Kim and Tracy in San Francisco
6. Antonio in San Diego
7. Kim and Tracy in Palm Springs
8. Kim and Tracy in Santa Barbara

KEY:
•—•—• Kim and Tracy's Trip
◆—◆—◆ Antonio's Trip

San Francisco
San Jose
Fresno
Santa Barbara
Los Angeles
Palm Springs
San Diego

C. How long does/did it take?

How long does it take to get to Los Angeles from Chicago?
It takes about four hours by plane.

How long did it take you to get to San Francisco from Los Angeles?
It took me eight hours by bus.

EXERCISE 10: *Complete the questions with* <u>How long does it take</u> *or* <u>How long did it take</u>.

1. A: _____ you to get to school yesterday?
   B: It took me ten minutes.

2. A: _____ to get from here to the nearest supermarket?
   B: It takes five minutes.

3. A: _____ you to get to the airport last night?
   B: It took us about an hour.

4. A: _____ you to get to your grandmother's house?
   B: It takes about four hours.

5. A: _____ you to get to New York by train?
   B: It takes less than two hours.

LISTENING

 EXERCISE 11: *Listen to the conversation. Fill in the chart about Samira's travel plans.*

From	To	Departure Time	Arrival Time	Travel By	Hours Traveled
New York City	London		6:25 A.M.	plane	
	Canterbury				
London	New York City				

 EXERCISE 12: *Listen to the conversation. Circle T or F for the correct answer.*

1. Samira wants to go to Italy. **T   F**
2. Samira wants to see the cathedral in Canterbury. **T   F**
3. The flight from New York to London takes six hours. **T   F**
4. Samira plans to fly from London to Canterbury. **T   F**
5. The train ride to Canterbury takes four hours. **T   F**
6. Samira will return to New York on May 30. **T   F**

SPEAKING

 EXERCISE 13: *Ask your partner the questions. Take turns.*

Where do you want to go on vacation?

Who do you want to go with?

What do you want to do there?

How do you want to get there?

EXERCISE 14: *Tell about your partner's answers in Exercise 13.*

(Partner's name) wants to go to _____ on **his/her** vacation. **He/she** wants to go by _____.

He/she wants to _____. **He/she** wants to go with _____.

READING

Look at the pictures. Read about Samira's vacation.

I started my vacation in London, England. Here I am at Windsor Castle. It's really huge! Someone took my picture when I was standing next to a guard in a funny hat. This day was a lot of fun.

After London, I went by train to Canterbury. I stayed in a little hotel that is 400 years old!

One morning I went to see the Canterbury Cathedral, one of the largest churches in England.

Stonehenge was my favorite place to visit in England. People built it about 4,000 years ago to watch the sun, moon, stars, and seasons. No one knows how the people built it, but . . .

EXERCISE 15: *Answer the questions about Samira's vacation.*

1. What country did Samira go to on her vacation?
2. What did she do at Windsor Castle?
3. How did Samira get to Canterbury?
4. How old was the hotel in Canterbury?
5. What was Samira's favorite place to visit in England?
6. Why do you think she liked her favorite place?

WRITING

EXERCISE 16: *Read the post card Samira wrote to her friend while she was on vacation. Pretend you're on vacation. Write a post card to a friend telling him or her about it.*

BRITISH MUSEUM: LONDON, ENGLAND
A famous landmark in London.

Dear Lucy,

How are you? I miss you, but I'm having a good time in England. This morning I went to the British Museum and saw many ancient objects. There was so much to see! I got tired and went to eat lunch and write letters. The food here is good, but I miss my mom's cooking at home. I'll buy a present for you while I'm here.

Samira

LONDON E.C.
8 MY
94
25

25ᴾ

Lucy Schneider

2204 W. Palmer Ave.

New York, NY 20001

U.S.A.

AIR MAIL

WARM UP

EXERCISE 1: *Answer the questions.*

1. How was Sylvia's weekend?
2. What did she want to do?
3. Why didn't she do it?
4. What kind of weather does Sylvia like for hiking?
5. Do you think Sylvia and Tracy can go hiking this weekend? Why or why not?

EXERCISE 2: *Answer the questions.*

1. What's the weather like when Tracy and Sylvia stop to rest?
2. What was the weather forecast?
3. Why did Sylvia and Tracy run to the car?
4. Why do you think Tracy wants the storm to end soon?
5. What does Sylvia think the weather will be like next?

VOCABULARY

What's the weather like?

 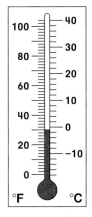

1. It's cold and snowy.   30°F / −1°C

 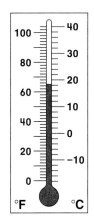

2. It's rainy and windy.   65°F / 18°C

 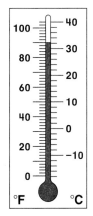

3. It's clear. It's hot and sunny too.   90°F / 32°C

 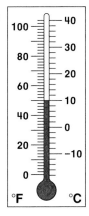

4. It's cool and windy.   50°F / 10°C

 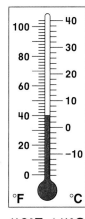

5. It's cloudy and cold.   40°F / 4°C

 EXERCISE 3: *Point to each picture. Ask and answer questions about the weather.*

A: What's the weather like?

B: It's cold and snowy.

---

clear   cold   rainy   stormy   windy
cloudy   hot   snowy   warm

1. _____

2. _____

3. _____

4. _____

5. _____

6. _____

7._____

8. _____

9. _____

WORD FOR WORD

Time Expressions

It was rainy and cold **last night.**
The weather is beautiful **today.**
It is going to be clear and 70° **tomorrow.**

Past	Future (going to)
yesterday	tomorrow
yesterday morning	tomorrow morning
yesterday afternoon	tomorrow afternoon
yesterday evening	tomorrow evening
last week	next week
last month	next month
last year	next year
last night	

 EXERCISE 5: *Write the correct word on the line.*

last	**today**	**yesterday**
next	**tomorrow**	

1. It's raining today but it's going to snow _____ .

2. It rained a lot _____ week.

3. It's raining _____ .

4. It's going to be sunny _____ afternoon.

5. It was very cold _____ . It's a little warmer today.

6. It's going to be hot _____ week. That's when I'm going to be on vacation.

 EXERCISE 6: *Read the weather forecast for the rest of Manuel's vacation. Then finish his postcard by using the words* <u>last</u>, <u>next</u>, <u>today</u>, *or* <u>tomorrow</u>.

W E A T H E R	Saturday, July 17
	Rainy and windy
	High: 78° Low: 65°

W E A T H E R	Sunday, July 18
	Cloudy and warm
	High: 80° Low: 68°

W E A T H E R	Wednesday, July 21
	Sunny and hot
	High: 90° Low: 72°

Saturday, July 17

Dear Grandma,

My vacation in Florida is great! **(1)**_____ *week, it was sunny every day. We played on the beach and read lots of books.* **(2)**_____ *it's rainy and the forecast says that* **(3)**_____ *it's going to be cloudy.* **(4)**_____ *Wednesday looks better—it's going to be sunny and hot again! I'll see you in a few more days!*

Love,
Manuel

Maria Hernández
7620 N. Paulina
Chicago, IL 60626

GRAMMAR

A. The Future Tense with Going To

What **are** you **going to do** tomorrow?	**I'm going to swim** in the ocean.
What **is** Ted **going to do**?	**He's going to hike** in the mountains.
What **is** the weather **going to be** like?	**It's going to rain** tonight. **I'm not going to** go out.
Where **are** you and Rita **going to be** tonight?	**We're going to be** at the dance.
Where **are** Ed and Barb **going to be**?	**They're going to be** at the dance too.

I'm going to = I am going to
He's going to = He is going to
We're going to = We are going to

I'm not going to = I am not going to
She's not going to = She is not going to
She isn't going to = She is not going to

EXERCISE 7: *What is everyone going to wear? Work with a partner. Ask and answer the questions. Use clothing words in your answers.*

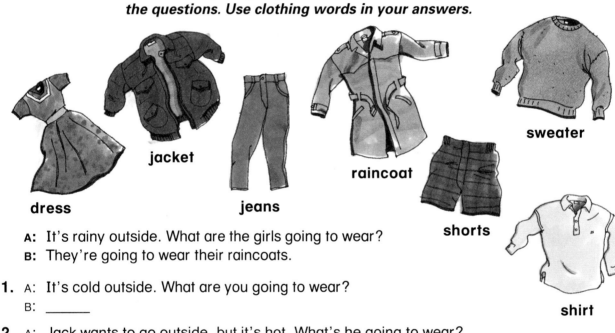

dress   **jacket**   jeans   **raincoat**   **shorts**   **sweater**

shirt

T-shirt

A: It's rainy outside. What are the girls going to wear?
B: They're going to wear their raincoats.

1. A: It's cold outside. What are you going to wear?
   B: _____

2. A: Jack wants to go outside, but it's hot. What's he going to wear?
   B: _____

3. A: What's María going to wear to the dance tomorrow?
   B: _____

4. A: What are you and your friend going to wear to the shopping mall?
   B: _____

5. (Ask another question with **you** and **going to wear**.)

EXERCISE 8: *Work with a partner. Ask and answer the questions. Take turns.*

1. What are you going to wear tomorrow?
2. What are you going to do tomorrow?
3. What are you going to do this weekend?
4. What are you going to do next week?

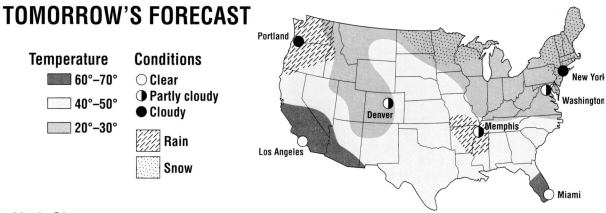

EXERCISE 9: *Work with a partner. Use the weather map and the city cues to ask and answer questions about the weather tomorrow. Take turns.*

TOMORROW'S FORECAST

Temperature
- 60°–70°
- 40°–50°
- 20°–30°

Conditions
- ○ Clear
- ◐ Partly cloudy
- ● Cloudy
- Rain
- Snow

New York City

A: What's the weather going to be like in New York City tomorrow?

B: It's going to be windy and cold.

1. Miami
2. Memphis
3. Denver
4. Portland
5. Los Angeles
6. Washington, D.C.

B. The Future Tense: Yes/No Questions with Going To

Is Lin **going to play** volleyball tonight?	Yes, she **is.**
Is the weather **going to be** nice tomorrow?	No, it **isn't.**
Are you **going to study** tonight?	No, **I'm not.**
Are your friends **going to be** at the game?	Yes, **they are.**

EXERCISE 10: *Write the correct words to complete the questions and answers.*

1. A: _____ it _____ be hot in New York City tomorrow?

   B: No, _____ .

2. A: _____ you _____ go to the bank at 2:00?

   B: Yes, _____ .

3. A: _____ Raúl and Teng _____ be at the movies?

   B: Yes, _____ .

4. A: _____ María _____ study tonight?

   B: No, _____ .

5. A: _____ Ted _____ play soccer this afternoon?

   B: Yes, _____ .

LISTENING

  EXERCISE 11: *Listen to the weather forecast. Circle the correct words.*

1. The weather in the morning is going to be   **sunny**   **rainy**   **cloudy.**

2. The weather in the afternoon is going to be   **rainy**   **sunny**   **warm.**

3. The high temperature this afternoon will be   **85°**   **65°**   **60°.**

4. The low temperature tonight will be   **40°**   **50°**   **55°.**

5. Tomorrow morning it is going to be   **sunny**   **rainy**   **cloudy.**

6. Tomorrow afternoon the skies will be   **cloudy**   **rainy**   **clear.**

7. The temperatures tomorrow evening are going to be   **warmer**   **colder**   **cooler.**

 SPEAKING

EXERCISE 12: *Ask your partner the questions. Take turns.*

EXERCISE 13: *Tell about your partner's answers in Exercise 12.*

____ likes to ____ when it's warm and sunny.
____ likes to ____ when it's rainy.
____ likes to ____ when it's cold and snowy.

 **READING**

WEATHER

CHICAGO: Today it is going to be warm and sunny in the morning and cool and rainy in the afternoon. The high temperature is going to be 82°. This evening it will be cool and cloudy, with the low temperature at around 60°. Tomorrow it is going to be windy and stormy in the morning. Tomorrow afternoon and evening it will be clear and cool. On Wednesday it's going to be sunny all day. The high temperature might reach 85°. The temperature on Wednesday evening will fall to around 70°. On Thursday, it is going to be hot all day. The high temperature might reach 90°. On Friday, it will be hot too, but it will start to cool off in the evening, when the temperature might fall to around 75°.

EXERCISE 14: *Read the weather report. Complete the chart.*

WEATHER FORECAST

	Morning	**Afternoon**	**Evening**
Today	*warm and sunny*		
Tomorrow			
Wednesday			
Thursday			
Friday			

EXERCISE 15: *Use the weather report and the chart to decide if each statement is true or false. Circle T or F.*

1. The high temperature is going to be 84° today.   T   F

2. The low tonight is going to be around 60°.   T   F

3. Tomorrow morning is going to be a good time to go swimming outside.   T   F

4. Tomorrow evening is going to be a good time to go to an outdoor baseball game.   T   F

5. Wednesday is going to be a good time to go hiking.   T   F

6. The low on Wednesday will be 85°.   T   F

7. Thursday will be a good time to fly a kite.   T   F

8. The low temperature will be around 75°.   T   F

WRITING

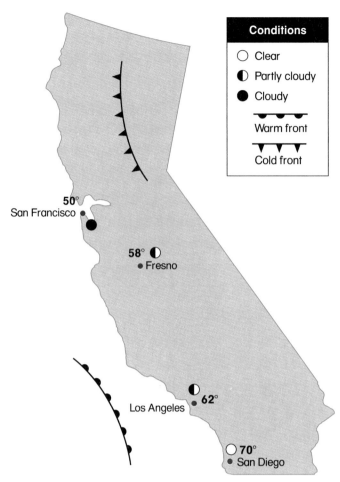

Conditions

○ Clear
◐ Partly cloudy
● Cloudy
~ ~ ~ Warm front
▼ ▼ ▼ Cold front

50° San Francisco ●

58° ◐ • Fresno

◐ • 62° Los Angeles

○ 70° • San Diego

 EXERCISE 16: *It's 8:00 in the morning. The map shows what the weather will be like in California this afternoon. Use the information on the map to write weather reports for the cities in the chart.*

City	Today's Weather Forecast
1. San Francisco	
2. Fresno	
3. Los Angeles	
4. San Diego	

EXERCISE 17: *Look at the chart in Exercise 16. Answer these questions with a partner.*

1. Which city would you like to go to today? Why?

2. Which city wouldn't you like to be in today? Why?

WARM UP

What are we going to do this afternoon?

We can watch TV.

It's raining! Why does it always rain when we have a school holiday?

1.

OK, Ed. What's on TV?

The Andy McCabe show is on at 3:00.

What kind of show is that?

I don't like talk shows. I usually watch only sports.

Well, there aren't any sports shows on now. There's a game show on Channel 4, a comedy on Channel 7, a movie on Channel 9, and a soap opera on Channel 12.

3.

It's a great talk show. Andy McCabe is the host. He has movie actors and actresses as his guests, and he asks them questions.

Let's watch the game show. That's my favorite kind of show.

2.

EXERCISE 1: _Answer the questions._

1. What's the weather like?
2. What are the people going to do?
3. What kinds of shows are on?
4. What kind of show are they going to watch?
5. What kind of show do you think Ed likes? Why?

4.

OK. It's not my favorite, but it's better than a soap opera!

VOCABULARY

A. What kind of TV show is it?

1. They're watching a comedy.

2. He's watching a commercial.

3. She's watching a drama.

4. They're watching the news.

5. They're watching a game show.

6. She's watching a soap opera.

7. They're watching a talk show.

8. They're watching a sports show.

EXERCISE 2: *Ask and answer the questions about the kinds of shows people are watching.*

A: What kind of show are they watching?

B: They're watching a comedy.

B. What does he do?

1.

She's an actress.　　He's an actor.

2.

He's the host.　　He's a game show contestant.

3.

She's a talk show host.　　He's a guest.

4.

She's a news reporter.

5.

He's an athlete.

EXERCISE 3: *Ask and answer questions about people on TV shows.*

A: What does he do?
B: He's an actor.

C. What's on TV?

TIME	CHANNEL 4	CHANNEL 5	CHANNEL 7
6:00	News	News	News
6:30		Life with Dad	The Liz Ames Show
7:00	NFL Football	The Samsons	Gold Rush
7:30		Never Again!	Win the Bank!
8:00		Police Stories	Movie: "Casablanca"
8:30			
9:00		Big Country	
9:30		Larry Jones Live	
10:00	News	News	News

TODAY'S TV PROGRAMS

 EXERCISE 4: *Ask and answer questions about the TV guide. Use the cues.*

Channel 4 / 6:00
A: What's on Channel 4 at 6:00?
B: News.

1. Channel 5 / 7:30
2. Channel 7 / 6:30
3. Channel 4 / 7:00
4. Channel 5 / 9:30
5. Channel 7 / 8:00

EXERCISE 5: *Ask and answer questions about different shows in the TV guide.*

A: What time does "Larry Jones Live" start?
B: It starts at 9:30.
A: What channel is it on?
B: It's on Channel 5.

actor	guest
actress	news
athlete	news reporter
commercial	soap opera
contestant	sports show
game show	~~talk show~~
game show host	talk show host

1. _talk show_

2. _____

3. _____

4. _____

5. _____

6. _____

WORD FOR WORD

At/In/On

When is "The Samsons" **on** TV?

Let's look **in** the TV guide. It's **on** the table.

"The Samsons" is **on** Wednesday **at** 7 o'clock.

EXERCISE 7: *Read the conversation. Write the correct word.*

at   in   on

1. A: What's _____ TV?

B: Let's see. Today's shows are listed _____ the TV guide.

2. A: Where's the TV guide?

B: It's _____ the table _____ the kitchen.

3. A: OK, _____ 4:30, we can watch news or cartoons.

B: Well, the news would tell us what's going on _____ the world.

4. A: But the cartoons would be more fun. What channel are they _____ ?

B: "Mighty Man" is _____ Channel 9. I'll turn it on.

5. A: What's _____ after "Mighty Man?"

B: There's news _____ 5:00 and 6:00.

6. A: And _____ 7:00, my favorite police show comes on!

B: That's right. Did you see the picture of the show's actor _____ the newspaper today? He won a prize.

GRAMMAR

Object Pronouns: Direct and Indirect Objects

Could you please give **me** the TV guide? I gave **you** the TV guide.	Could you please give the TV guide to **me**? I gave it to **you.**
Did Ken give **her** the book? No, she gave **him** the book.	Did Ken give the book to **her**? No, she gave it to **him.**
Did Pam and Lucy show **you** the pictures? Yes, they showed **us** the pictures. We showed **them** some pictures, too.	Did Pam and Lucy show the pictures to **you**? Yes, they showed the pictures to **us.** We showed some pictures to **them,** too.

EXERCISE 8: *Work with a partner. Use the cues to ask questions. Take turns asking and answering.*

you / give / me / the TV guide
A: Could you please give me the TV guide?
B: Sure. Here it is.

1. you / show / your pictures / to him
2. you / tell / me / a story
3. you / give / her / the book
4. you / show / us / the pictures
5. you / give / the TV guide / to them
6. you / ask / him / about / the pictures

EXERCISE 9: *Read. Write the correct word or words.*

1. The news reporter asked _____ a question.
her / to her

2. She didn't give _____ an answer.
him / to him

3. The game show host showed _____ a giant TV set.
us / to us

4. The Simpsons don't have a TV, so we're going to give one _____ .
them / to them

5. The sports reporter told _____ a great story.
us / to us

6. The librarian showed the book _____ .
me / to me

LISTENING

 EXERCISE 10: *Listen to the commercials. Circle the answers.*

Commercial 1

1. This commercial is for
   a. a radio show.
   b. a restaurant.
   c. a television show.

2. "Sunny Skies" is a
   a. talk show.
   b. comedy.
   c. sports show.

Commercial 2

3. This commercial is selling
   a. food.
   b. clothing.
   c. music.

4. The Pita Shack is a
   a. music store.
   b. drugstore.
   c. restaurant.

Commercial 3

5. This commercial is for
   a. blue jeans.
   b. basketball shoes.
   c. basketballs.

6. The brand name is
   a. Sky High.
   b. Mile High.
   c. High School.

 SPEAKING

 EXERCISE 11: *Work with a partner. Talk about what you watched on TV. Take turns.*

UNIT 10   WHAT'S YOUR FAVORITE SHOW?

EXERCISE 12: *Tell about your partner in Exercise 11.*

1. This is _____ .
2. **He / She** watched _____ last week.
3. **He / She** liked _____ best.
4. It was about _____ .

READING

WHAT HAPPENED ON THE SOAPS?

The Good Life

MONDAY

Monica was finally home alone. She packed her suitcases. She wrote a note to her parents saying that she was going to New York City to be an actress. Then she called a taxi and left for the bus station.

Carmen got home and couldn't find Monica. Then she found the note and cried. Next she called her sister Teresa in New York City to tell her about Monica.

When Adam came home from work, Carmen showed him the note. He was angry at Carmen because she wanted their daughter to be an actress.

TUESDAY

Carmen and Adam talked more about Monica. Adam finally realized that Carmen didn't cause their daughter to leave. Teresa called late at night to say that she got a call from Monica. Monica was at the bus station in Chicago because there was a snowstorm there and the roads were closed.

EXERCISE 13: *Read about "The Good Life." Ask and answer the questions with a partner.*

1. What kind of show is it?
2. Who is on the show?
3. What happened?
4. What do you think will happen next?

WRITING

EXERCISE 14: *List in the chart all the TV shows you watch for the next two days.*

Day	Time Show Starts	TV Show	How Long?
Monday	7:00	Star Power	30 minutes

EXERCISE 15: *Write about what happened in one of the shows you listed in Exercise 14.*

Name of show: _____

Kind of show: _____

This is what happened on the show:

_____

_____

_____

_____

_____

_____

_____

_____

_____

_____

_____

UNIT 11 Who Won the Game?

WARM UP

Wow! Hockey looks dangerous! Did you see that player fall?

It's exciting, Tony! That team just made a run. The Hawks are winning three to two.

No, Ayo. That team made a goal. Runs are points in baseball.

Points in soccer are called goals too.

Yes, I know. Soccer is a popular game in Nigeria.

Do you play soccer, Ayo?

Yes. It's my favorite sport.

What's your favorite sport?

I like to play basketball.

I like to go skiing.

I like to go swimming.

1.

2.

3.

4.

EXERCISE 1: *Answer the questions.*

1. What sport are Ayo and his friends watching?
2. Why does Tony think that hockey is dangerous?
3. What sport is popular in Nigeria?
4. What sports do Ayo's friends like?

EXERCISE 2: *Answer the questions.*

1. What does Jane want to do?
2. What doesn't Ayo know how to do?
3. How will Ayo learn to ice skate?
4. How do you stop on ice skates?
5. Do you think Ayo likes to skate? Why or why not?

V VOCABULARY

A. What's the score?

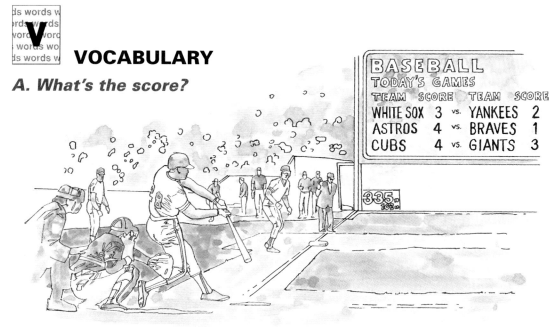

BASEBALL
TODAY'S GAMES

TEAM	SCORE		TEAM	SCORE
WHITE SOX	3	VS.	YANKEES	2
ASTROS	4	VS.	BRAVES	1
CUBS	4	VS.	GIANTS	3

EXERCISE 3: *Ask and answer questions about the games.*

A: What's the score of the White Sox game?
B: The White Sox are winning three to two.

A: What's the score of the Yankees game?
B: The Yankees are losing three to two.

B. Did they win?

Bulls	110
Knicks	98

Lakers	92
Suns	103

Nets	90
Pacers	94

EXERCISE 4: *Ask and answer questions about the games.*

A: Did the Bulls win?
B: Yes, they won 110 to 98.

A: Did the Knicks win?
B: No, they lost 110 to 98.

C. That looks dangerous!

1. I think that bike riding is fun.

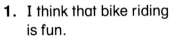

2. I think that playing chess is interesting.

3. I think that ice skating is exciting.

4. I think that tennis is fun.

5. I think that playing hockey is dangerous.

6. I think that golf is boring.

7. I think that swimming is easy.

8. I think that learning a new sport is hard.

EXERCISE 5: *What do the people in the pictures think about their activities? Complete each sentence with the best word.*

boring	easy	fun	interesting
dangerous	exciting	hard	popular

1. He thinks that skiing is _____ .

2. They think that dancing is _____.

3. They think that chess is _____ to play.

4. The people watching the game think that soccer is _____.

5. He thinks that golf is _____ to play.

7. She thinks that basketball is _____ to play.

6. She thinks that ice skating is _____ .

WORD FOR WORD

Go + -ing *Words*

He likes to **go shopping.**	shop + ing = shopping
They are **going skiing.**	ski + ing = skiing
We **went skating.**	skat~~e~~ + ing = skating

 EXERCISE 6: *Write* <u>go</u> *and an* <u>-ing</u> *word on the line.*

dance	run	ski
ride	shop	swim

1. In the winter, I like to _____ in the mountains.

2. On Saturday nights my friends and I _____.

3. Zola and Allen like to _____ after work.

4. In the afternoons, our neighbors like to _____.

5. I like to _____ on weekends.

6. We _____ every Saturday.

GRAMMAR

A. It's + Infinitive

> It's fun **to ice skate**.
> It's exciting **to play** hockey.
> I think **it's** hard **to learn** a new sport.

EXERCISE 7: *Work with a partner. Partner A makes a sentence with the words. Partner B agrees or disagrees. Take turns.*

hard / play tennis

A: It's hard to play tennis.
B: I agree.   OR   I think it's easy to play tennis.

1. easy / play soccer
2. fun / play hockey
3. exciting / play basketball
4. interesting / ski
5. boring / play chess
6. hard / swim

EXERCISE 8: *Work with a partner. Ask questions about the actions in the pictures. Answer with your own opinions, using any of these words. Take turns.*

boring	easy	fun	interesting
dangerous	exciting	hard	

A: Do you like to read books about real people?
B: Yes, it's interesting to read them.

1.

2.

3.

4.

5

6.

B. -ing Words as Nouns

Swimming is fun on a hot day.
I like **swimming** in the ocean.
Does Greg like downhill **skiing**?
No, he thinks **skiing** is dangerous.

 EXERCISE 9: *Make questions using -ing words as nouns. Circle your partner's answers. Then circle your answers. Do you like doing the same things?*

A: Do you like listening to rock music?
B: Yes, I do. Do you?
A: Not really.

	Does My Partner Like...?		Do I Like...?	
1. listen to rock music	Yes	No	Yes	No
2. ride a bike	Yes	No	Yes	No
3. swim in the ocean	Yes	No	Yes	No
4. play baseball	Yes	No	Yes	No
5. play soccer	Yes	No	Yes	No
6. shop in the mall	Yes	No	Yes	No
7. play chess	Yes	No	Yes	No
8. ice skate	Yes	No	Yes	No

C. Let's

Let's **go** to the movies.
Let's **have** lunch.
Let's **go** ice skating.

EXERCISE 10: *Read each sentence. What do you want to do? Tell your partner.*

It's windy.
Let's fly a kite.

1. It snowed last night.
2. It's raining.
3. We need milk and eggs.
4. I've got a great new CD.
5. It's hot today.
6. I'm hungry.

LISTENING

 EXERCISE 11: *Listen to the conversation. Circle the correct words.*

1. First, Dan wants to go   skating   shopping   swimming.
2. Lisa thinks skating is   exciting   dangerous   boring.
3. Then, Dan wants to go   skiing   bike riding   swimming.
4. Lisa likes   **sailing**   bike riding   skating.
5. Dan thinks sailing is   **fun**   boring   hard.

water skiing

 EXERCISE 12: *Who wants to do what? Listen to the conversation. Put an X in the box. Then put an X under You for each activity you'd like to do.*

	Dan	**Lisa**	**You**
sailing			
bike riding			
water skiing			
swimming			
skating			
wind surfing			

windsurfing

sailing

 # SPEAKING

EXERCISE 13: *Ask your partner the questions. Take turns.*

What's your favorite sport?

Why is it your favorite?

What sports are you good at?

What is your favorite sports team?

EXERCISE 14: *Tell about your partner's answers in Exercise 13.*

_____ 's favorite sport is _____ .

_____ is **his**/**her** favorite sport because _____ .

_____ is good at _____ .

_____ is **his**/**her** favorite team.

UNIT 11   WHO WON THE GAME?   113

READING

Tigers Win Soccer Game

In an exciting win over the Westville Wildcats Saturday, the Central High School girls soccer team showed that victory is sweet.

The final score was 6 to 3. Star player María Hernández scored two goals and had four assists.

María Hernández

When asked what makes her a great soccer player she said, "I love soccer. It's my favorite sport! Soccer practice doesn't feel like work. It's too much fun!"

The Tigers are going to play the undefeated Park Forest Patriots next Tuesday. If they can win that game, they will play in the state championship.

victory:

undefeated:

championship:

 EXERCISE 15: *Read the sports article. Answer the questions.*

1. Who won the soccer game Saturday?
2. Who did the Tigers play against?
3. Who is the star player of the Tigers?
4. Why is she a good soccer player?
5. What do the Tigers have to do to get to the state championship?

 # WRITING

 EXERCISE 16: *Write about a game you played or watched other people play. Who won? What was the score?*

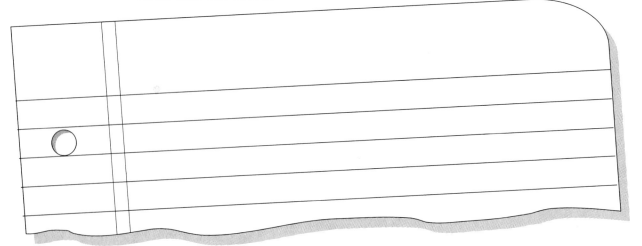

WARM UP

EXERCISE 1: *Answer the questions.*

1. What are the students going to work on?
2. Who's going to write about sports?
3. Who's going to draw and write the comics?
4. What kinds of events do you think Reiko can write about?

V VOCABULARY

A. What part of the newspaper are you looking at?

1. front page
2. headline
3. article
4. photograph
5. column
6. ad (advertisement)
7. comic strip

The
Lion's Roar

Friday   ★★★★★

Lions Win Big Game

In an exciting win over the Westville Wildcats Saturday, the Central High School girls soccer team showed that victory is sweet.

The final score was 4 to 3. Star player Maria Hernandez scored two goals and had four assists. When asked what makes her a great soccer player she said, "I love soccer. It's my favorite

...me, they will play in the ...te championship.

How does coach feel? ...ach Rooney said, "It ...as an exciting game. I ...ink we can win the

...district championship next week."

If the Tigers can win that game, they will play in the state championship. How does the Tiger's chances

Page 7

The Lion's Roar

March of the Snow People

Nancy's Advice

Dear Nancy,
My friends always come to my house after school. My mother doesn't want them to come here any more because she doesn't like the music we listen to. What can I do?
                    Worried

Dear Worried,
Ask your friends if you can go to their houses. Try not to play the music very loud.
                    Nancy

Classifieds

FOR SALE: Used bike $5 3spd boys, green. hand brakes

Like new 1993 car, 4dr p/b, p/s

Lawnmower for sale $35.

2 pair of new rollerskates. Still in box! $40.

Come to the

Pep Club
Bake Sale!

EXERCISE 2: *Ask and answer questions about the newspaper.*

A: What part of the newspaper are you looking at?
B: The front page.

B. What's this?

Movie Review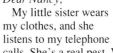
by Mike Plotsky

"Big Bang" a Bust!

"Big Bang" is at the Bijou movie theater. The movie stars Miranda Marvel and Harvey Schwartz. It's about police in a big city.

This movie is terrible. Don't go see it.

Nancy's Advice

Dear Nancy,
My little sister wears my clothes, and she listens to my telephone calls. She's a real pest. What can I do?
Angry Annie

Dear Angry Annie,
Give her your old clothes and a music CD she likes. She might stop bugging you.
Nancy

 EXERCISE 3: *Ask and answer the questions.*

1. What's the movie review about?
2. What's the advice column about?

C. What do they do?

1. She's a reporter.
She finds out the news.

2. He's an editor.
He corrects mistakes.

3. He's a photographer.
He takes pictures.

4. She's a writer.
She writes articles.

5. She's a cartoonist.
She draws and writes comics.

 EXERCISE 4: *Ask and answer questions about what the people do for the newspaper.*

A: What does she do?
B: She's a reporter. She finds out the news.

---

ad column editor photographer review
article comic strip headline reporter writer

Janna's Advice

by Janna Benson

Dear Janna,

People are always angry at me because I never arrive anywhere on time. What can I do?

FOR SALE:
Skates. Like new. $25.00. Call 555-1212.

Clara Barton is a book about the woman who started the American Red Cross.

It's a great story about an interesting woman. **Read it!**

1. _____   2. _____   3. _____

Mom, this is my new friend, Elliot.

Jets Win Championship!

Last night the Hampton High School Jets won their first championship in ten years. The coach congratulated the players and showed them their trophy. Tomorrow at noon there is going to be a victory parade on

Morton High Jazz Band Gives Concert

4. _____   5. _____   6. _____

7. _____   8. _____   9. _____

WORD FOR WORD
Location Words

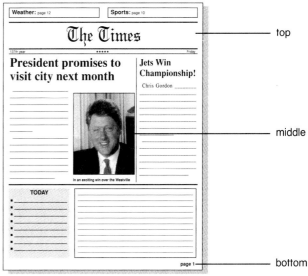

The important news is **on the front page.**
The headline is **at the top of the page.**
The page number is **at the bottom of the page.**
The photograph is **in the middle of the page.**
The sports article is **in the second column.**
My name is **on the first line in the last column.**

EXERCISE 6: *Look at the newspaper page. Complete the sentence with the correct location words from the box at the top of the page.*

1. The photograph is _____ .

2. The headline about the hospital is _____ .

3. The article about the mayor's election is _____ .

4. The page number is _____ .

5. The ad is _____ .

6. The article about the President is _____ .

7. The comic strip is _____ .

EXERCISE 7: *Work with a partner. Ask and answer questions about the newspaper page above.*

A: Where's the headline about the hospital?
B: It's in the first column, near the bottom of the page.

G GRAMMAR

A. Verb Tense Review

Present Progressive	Are you **writing** your newspaper article now?
Simple Past	No, but I **wrote** the first paragraph last night.
Simple Present	But you **work** on the newspaper every Monday, Tuesday, and Wednesday.
Infinitive	I know. But today I want **to work** on my science project.
Future	I'm **going to write** my newspaper article on Thursday.

EXERCISE 8: *Read. Circle the correct words.*

Yolanda Cruz **(1)** has / had an interesting vacation last month. She **(2)** went / goes to New York City.

While she was there, she **(3)** visited / is visiting the Metropolitan Museum of Art, the Modern Museum

of Art, and the Statue of Liberty. She also went **(4)** to see / saw two actors from the TV show, "The

Young and the Beautiful."

Yolanda's favorite place **(5)** is going to be / was the

Modern Museum of Art because she wants

(6) to be / is an artist. She **(7)** draws / to draw pictures

every day. She **(8)** is going to show / to draw her

drawings at the art fair next Saturday.

B. Verb Tense Review: Questions and Answers

Is Maria **writing** the sports column now?	Yes, she **is**.
Did it **rain** last night?	No, it **didn't**.
Were you at the dance last night?	No, I **wasn't**.
Does Kenji usually go to school dances?	Yes, he **does**.
Is he tall and thin?	No, he **isn't**.
Are Kenji and Alma **going to be** here tomorrow?	No, they **aren't**.

EXERCISE 9: *Read the question. Write the letter of the answer on the line. Watch the verb tenses.*

1. Did you go to the concert last night? _____   **a.** Yes, I am.

2. Was Maria at the concert? _____   **b.** Yes, it is.

3. Do Peter and Teng often play Frisbee? _____   **c.** No, I didn't.

4. Is it going to rain tonight? _____   **d.** Yes, they are.

5. Are you listening to the radio? _____   **e.** No, she wasn't.

6. Are Pedro and his brother at home? _____   **f.** Yes, they do.

How **was** your vacation in Florida?	It **was** great!
When **did** you and your family **go** there?	We **went** there last week.
Where **does** Lin usually **go** after school?	She usually **goes** home.
Why **isn't** Fred **going to be** in class?	He's **going to go** to the dentist's office.

EXERCISE 10: *Complete the conversation with the correct form of each verb.*

MEI: Hi, Rosa. How **(1. be)** _____ you?

ROSA: Fine. What **(2. do)** _____ you _____ last night?

MEI: I **(3. play)** _____ volleyball. Why **(4. be, neg.)** _____ you at the game?

ROSA: I **(5. be)** _____ sick with the flu yesterday.

MEI: That's too bad. What **(6. do)** _____ you _____ next weekend?

ROSA: I **(7. work)** _____ next Saturday. My father always **(8. ask)** _____ me to work in his store on weekends.

MEI: We **(9. go shopping)** _____ next Saturday. Maybe we can visit you in your store!

LISTENING

EXERCISE 11: *Listen to the news reports. Write the number of the news report next to the headline it matches.*

___LIONS WIN!   ___SUNNY WEATHER TOMORROW

___Reggie's Movie Reviews   ___CAR ACCIDENT DOWNTOWN

EXERCISE 12: *Listen to the news reports again. Circle the answer to each question.*

1. The car accident happened
   a. yesterday morning.
   b. last night.
   c. this morning.

2. Tonight the weather is going to be
   a. rainy and cool.
   b. windy and cold.
   c. warm and sunny.

3. The Lions played the Tigers.
   a. last week.
   b. last night.
   c. last year.

4. The score was
   a. Lions 62, Tigers 55.
   b. Lions 72, Tigers 65.
   c. Tigers 82, Lions 65.

5. "Lost in Alaska" is at
   a. the Orion Cinema.
   b. the Cinemax Theater.
   c. the Regal Theater.

6. The two men in the movie
   a. get lost in the mountains.
   b. drive a car across the country.
   c. play basketball.

SPEAKING

EXERCISE 13: *Ask your partner the questions. Take turns.*

READING

A news reporter asks these questions:
Who?   What?   Where?   When?   How?

Read the newspaper article by Jim Adams.

Mr. Smith's Class Welcomes New Student
by Jim Adams

Teresa Salazar is a new student at Central High School. Teresa is from the Philippines. She and her family moved to the United States last month. Mr. Smith's class had a party to welcome Teresa. Her hobbies are swimming, bike riding, dancing, and reading. Teresa said she misses her friends in the Philippines, but she is happy to be in the United States.

 EXERCISE 14: *Fill in Jim's notes for the article.*

Notes about New Student

Who (name)? _____

What is special about her? _____

Where from? _____ When? _____

How does she feel about moving? _____

Interests? _____

Players Off To A Good Start
by Melba Sanders

The school drama club, The Players, held their first meeting of the year on September 9. Twenty-one members met in the auditorium.

At this first meeting, club officers were elected. Sophia Levi will be the new president. Mark Griffin will be secretary/treasurer. The club sponsor is Ms. Foster.

Ms. Foster announced that the club will perform "The Quest" this year. The play is a drama about the Gold Rush. All students in the school are invited to help.

 EXERCISE 15: *Fill in Melba's notes for the article.*

What? _____ When? _____ How many? _____

Who? President _____

       Secretary/Treasurer _____

       Sponsor _____

What play? _____ Subject? _____

Who is invited? _____

WRITING

Read Kim's notes for a sports article.

Notes About Soccer Game

Who? Lions and Jefferson High School Tigers

When? Last Friday

Where? Lincoln High School

What Score? Lions 4, Tigers 3

How does coach feel? Coach Rooney said, "It was an exciting game. I think we can win the district championship next week."

EXERCISE 16: *Use Kim's notes. Write a sports article about the Lions.*

EXERCISE 17: *You and your classmates can write a newspaper. Write a name for it.*

EXERCISE 18: *What do you want to write for your class newspaper? Circle one item.*

1. an ad

2. a comic strip

3. an article

    a. news   **b.** sports

4. an advice column

5. a weather report

6. a review

    a. book   **b.** movie   **c.** music   **d.** TV

EXERCISE 19: *On a sheet of paper, make notes about what you will write for your newspaper.*

THE INTERNATIONAL PHONETIC ALPHABET

IPA SYMBOLS

CONSONANTS

/b/	**b**a**b**y, clu**b**
/d/	**d**own, to**d**ay, sa**d**
/f/	**f**un, pre**f**er, lau**gh**
/g/	**g**ood, be**g**in, do**g**
/h/	**h**ome, be**h**ind
/k/	**k**ey, cho**c**olate, bla**ck**
/l/	**l**ate, po**l**ice, mai**l**
/m/	**m**ay, wo**m**an, swi**m**
/n/	**n**o, opi**n**ion
/ŋ/	a**ng**ry, lo**ng**
/p/	**p**a**p**er, ma**p**
/r/	**r**ain, pa**r**ent, doo**r**
/s/	**s**alt, medi**c**ine, bu**s**
/š/	**s**ugar, **s**pecial, fi**sh**
/t/	**t**ea, ma**t**erial, da**t**e
/θ/	**th**ing, heal**th**y, ba**th**
/ð/	**th**is, mo**th**er, ba**th**e
/v/	**v**ery, tra**v**el, o**f**
/w/	**w**ay, any**o**ne
/y/	**y**es, oni**o**n
/z/	**z**oo, cou**s**in, alway**s**
/ž/	mea**s**ure, gara**g**e
/č/	**ch**eck, pi**c**ture, wa**tch**
/ĵ/	**j**ob, refri**g**erator, oran**g**e

VOWELS

/ɑ/	**o**n, h**o**t, f**a**ther
/æ/	**a**nd c**a**sh
/ɛ/	**e**gg, s**ay**s, l**ea**ther
/ɪ/	**i**n, b**i**g
/ɔ/	**o**ff, d**au**ghter, dr**aw**
/e/	**A**pril, tr**ai**n, s**ay**
/i/	**e**ven, sp**ea**k, tr**ee**
/o/	**o**pen, cl**o**se, sh**ow**
/u/	b**oo**t, d**o**, thr**ough**
/ʌ/	**o**f, y**ou**ng, s**u**n
/ʊ/	p**u**t, c**oo**k, w**ou**ld
/ə/	**a**bout, penc**i**l, lem**o**n
/ɚ/	moth**er**, Satur**d**ay, doct**or**
/ɝ/	**ear**th, b**ur**n, h**er**

Diphthongs

/ɑɪ/	**i**ce, st**y**le, l**ie**
/ɑʊ/	**ou**t, d**ow**n, h**ow**
/ɔɪ/	**oi**l, n**oi**se, b**oy**

THE ENGLISH ALPHABET

Here is the pronunciation of the letters of the English alphabet, written in International Phonetic Alphabet Symbols.

a	/e/
b	/bi/
c	/si/
d	/di/
e	/i/
f	/ɛf/
g	/ĵi/
h	/eč/
i	/ɑɪ/
j	/ĵe/
k	/ke/
l	/ɛl/
m	/ɛm/
n	/ɛn/
o	/o/
p	/pi/
q	/kyu/
r	/ɑr/
s	/ɛs/
t	/ti/
u	/yu/
v	/vi/
w	/ˈdʌbəlˌyu/
x	/ɛks/
y	/wɑɪ/
z	/zi/

VOCABULARY

Arabic numbers indicate units in On Your Mark 2.
GS indicates "Getting Started." I indicates On Your Mark 1.

about   10
accident   5
across (from)   I
ad   12
address   I
after   3
afternoon   3
airport   8
always   I
am   I
ambulance   5
answer   I
apple   2
April   GS
are   I
area code   I
arm   I
art   I
article   12
ask   I
assembly   6
attend   6
auditorium   6
August   GS
average   7
awful   2

back   I
backache   I
ball   I
ballet   8
banana   2
band   I
bank   I
baseball   I
basketball   I
beach   8
before   3
between   I
big   I
bike   I
birthday   GS
black   I
bleeding   5
blue   I
board   I

book   I
book bag   I
border (on)   8
boring   11
borrow   I
bottle   I
bottom   12
bowl   I
boy   I
bread   2
break   5
break into   5
breakfast   3
breathing   5
brother   I
brown   I
brush   4
brush teeth   3
burglar   5
bus   I
bus driver   I
bus stop   4
buy   I

cafeteria   I
cake   1
calendar   1
can/can't   I
candles   1
carrot   2
carton   I
cartoonist   12
cashier   I
catch   I
chair   I
chalk   I
celebrate   1
cheer   6
cheese   I
cheeseburger   I
chicken   I
choking   5
circle   I
class   I
clear   9
close (verb)   I

clothing store   I
cloudy   9
cold   9
color   I
column   12
comb   4
comb hair   4
come   1
comedy   10
comic strip   12
commercial   20
compact disc (CD)   4
computer   I
concert   6
contestant   10
cook   I
cool   9
corner   I
cost   I
count   I
cup   I
curly   7

dance   6
dangerous   11
date   1
daughter   I
day   1
December   GS
decorate   6
decorations   1
delicious   2
deliver   I
dentist   I
desk   I
dinner   3
directions   8
do/does   I
door   I
drama   10
draw   I
drive   I
drugstore   I

early   3
east   8

easy   11
editor   12
egg   2
eight   I
eighteen   I
eighteenth   1
eighth   1
eighty   I
election   6
eleven   I
eleventh   1
emergency   5
enter   7
eraser   I
evening   3
exciting   11
eyes   6

fall   5
father   I
February   GS
feel   I
fifteen   I
fifteenth   1
fifth   1
fifty   I
find   I
finger   I
fire   I
fire station   I
firefighter   I
first   1
fish   2
five   I
fix   I
fly   8
foot   I
forty   I
four   I
fourteen   I
fourteenth   1
fourth   1
French fries   I
Friday   I
friend   1
front page   12

fruit 2
fun 11

game 6
game show 10
garage 5
gas 4
gas station 4
get 1
get dressed 3
get home 3
get up 3
girl I
give 1
glasses 7
go I
go to bed 3
goals 11
good 2
good-by I
grandfather I
grandmother I
grapes 2
great I
green I
grocery store 4
guest 10
gym I

hair 7
half-past I
hand I
happen 5
happy I
hard 11
hardly 5
have/has I
he/he's I
head I
headache I
headline 12
heavy 7
height 7
hello I
help I
her I
hi I
hike 9
his I
hit I
holiday 1
homework I
hospital I
host 10
hot 9
hot dog I
hotel 8
how much I
hungry I
hurt I
husband I

ice cream 1
I'm I
in I
interesting 11
invite 1
its I
it's I

jacket I
January GS
jeans I
job I
July GS
June GS

keep order I
kick I

large I
last (week) 9
late 3
learn I
leave 3
left I
leg I
letter I
librarian I
library I
like I
line I
listen I
live GS
locker I
look 2
look for I
look like 7
lose 11
lunch I

magazine 4
mail I
mail carrier I
make I
mall I
man/men I
March GS
march (verb) 6
match I
math I
May GS
medium I
meeting 6
middle 12
milk I
Monday I
month GS
morning 3
mother I
motorcycle 8
mountains 8
movie theater 4
movies I

museum 8
music I
music store 4
my I

name I
near I
need I
neighbor 5
never I
news 10
newspaper 4
next (month) 9
next (to) I
nice 7
night 3
nine I
nineteen I
nineteenth 1
ninety I
ninth 1
noon 3
north 8
notebook I
November GS
number I
nurse I

ocean 8
o'clock I
October GS
office I
often 1
on I
on fire I
one I
one hundred I
open (verb) I
orange (color) I
orange (noun) 2
order I
our I

page I
paper I
parents I
park I
party 1
past I
P.E. teacher I
peas 2
pen I
pencil I
people I
phone number I
photograph 12
photographer 12
physical education I
pick up I
picture I
piece I
pink I

pizza I
play I
point to I
points 11
police officer I
police station I
pool I
popular 11
post office I
potato 2
practice I
present 1
president 6
pretty 7
principal I
purple I
purse 5
put out I

(a) quarter to/after I

rain 9
rainy 9
raise I
read I
red I
rent (verb) 4
reporter 10
rest room I
restaurant I
review 12
rice 2
ride I
right I
run I
run for (office) 6
run into 5

sad I
salad I
salesperson I
sandwich I
Saturday I
sausage I
schedule I
science I
science fair 6
second 1
secretary 6
section 12
see 5
sell I
September GS
seven I
seventeen I
seventeenth 1
seventh 1
seventy I
she/she's I
shirt I
shoes I
shop 4

sick   I
sing   I
sister   I
sit down   I
six   I
sixteen   I
sixteenth   1
sixth   1
sixty   I
skate   I
skirt   I
slice   I
small   I
smell   2
snack   3
snow   9
snowy   9
soap opera   10
soccer   I
social studies   I
sometimes   1
son   I
sore throat   I
south   8
spell   I
sports show   10
stand up   I
steal   5
stomach   I
stomachache   I
storm   9
stormy   9
straight (ahead)   7
street   I
student   I
student council   6
study   I
Sunday   I
sunny   9

supermarket   I
sweater   I
swim   I

table   I
take   I
take a bus   6
take a shower   3
take a vacation   8
talk   10
talk show   10
tall   7
tape   4
taste   2
teach   I
teacher   I
team   6
teeth   I
ten   I
tenth   1
terrible   I
their   I
there are   1
there is   1
these   I
they/they're   I
thin   7
third   1
thirsty   I
thirteen   I
thirteenth   1
thirtieth   1
thirty   I
thirty-first   1
three   I
throat   I
throw   I
Thursday   I
time   I

tired   I
toe   I
tomato   2
tomorrow   9
too   I
toothbrush   4
toothpaste   4
top   12
train   8
travel   8
treasurer   6
truck   5
T-shirt   I
Tuesday   I
turn   I
TV guide   10
twelfth   1
twelve   I
twentieth   1
twenty   I
twenty-eighth   1
twenty-fifth   1
twenty-first   1
twenty-fourth   1
twenty-ninth   1
twenty-second   1
twenty-seventh   1
twenty-sixth   1
twenty-third   1
two   I

unconscious   5
under   I
usually   1

vacation   8
vegetable   I
vice-president   6
video   4

video store   4
vote   6

wait for   4
walk   I
wallet   5
want   I
warm   9
wastebasket   I
we   I
wear   I
weather   9
Wednesday   I
weekend   I
weight   7
west   8
what/what's   I
what time   I
What's the matter?   I
when   I
where/where's   I
white   I
who/who's   I
wife   I
win   11
window   I
windy   9
woman/women   I
word   I
would you like   I
write   I

year   1
yellow   I
you   I
your   I
zero   I

Unit 1

We **always** stay home from school on Martin Luther King Day. Do you **usually** go to school on Groundhog Day? Yes, but we **never** go to school on Saturday or Sunday.	
Does your teacher **often** tell you about holidays? Yes, he does. He **sometimes** celebrates holidays with us too.	

There **is** a holiday in May. **Is there** a holiday in September? **Is there** a holiday this Monday?	Yes, **there is.** No, **there isn't.** No, **there's not.**
There **are** thirty days in June. **Are there** thirty days in September? **Are there** thirty days in February?	Yes, **there are.** No, **there aren't.**

Unit 2

How many apples do you want? **How many potatoes** do you want?	One, please. Two, please.
How much beef do you want? **How much soup** do you want?	Two slices, please. A cup, please.

The fish **looks** good. These grapes **taste** delicious. This milk **smells** awful.

Unit 3

I eat breakfast at 7:30 in the morning. I go to school at 8:00 in the morning.	**Before** I go to school, I eat breakfast. **After** I eat breakfast, I go to school.

Do you and Sue **have to** go home now? **Does** Jason **have to** do his homework now?	No, we **don't.** We **don't have to** go home until 8:00. Yes, he **does.**
What **do** you **have to** do today? What **does** Lin **have to** do today?	I **have to go** to the dentist. She **has to go** to the drugstore.

Unit 4

Where **does** Ruben **want to go?** Why **does** he **want to go** there?	He **wants to go** to the music store. Because he **needs to buy** a tape.
Do you **want to rent** a video? **Does** Mei **need to go** to the bank?	Yes, I **want to rent** "Jurassic Park." No, she **doesn't need to go** there.

What **are** you doing now? Where **is** Tara going? **Are** you **making** pizza?	I'm **making** dinner She's **going** to the bank. Yes, I **am.**	What **do** you **do** on Monday nights? What **does** Rex **want** for dinner? **Do** you **like** carrots?	I **go** to band practice. He **wants** a pizza. No, I **don't.**

Unit 5

Regular Verbs	
The Simple Present Tense	**The Simple Past Tense**
I always **call** 911 in an emergency. Accidents sometimes **happen** here.	Yesterday, I **called** 911. This morning an accident **happened** on our street.

Irregular Verbs	
The Simple Present Tense	**The Simple Past Tense**
I sometimes **break** things. Marta sometimes **falls** down. We sometimes **see** accidents. Trucks sometimes **hit** cars. Ben sometimes **takes** the bus. Burglars often **steal** things. Jenny **runs** every morning. I usually **get** groceries on Thursdays. We usually **go** to Rob's Grocery.	I **broke** a window yesterday. She **fell** down last night. We **saw** a car accident yesterday. A truck **hit** a car this morning. Ben **took** the bus last night. A burglar **stole** our TV set last night. This morning she **ran** for half an hour. This week, I **got** groceries on Friday. On Friday, we **went** to Best Grocery.

What **did** you **see?** Where **did** it **happen?** When **did** it **happen?** How **did** it **happen?**	I **saw** an accident. A blue car **hit** a green car. It **happened** in front of my school. It **happened** at about 3 o'clock today. The green car **turned** left on a red light.

Unit 6

Did you **study** for your math test? **Did** you **talk** to Inés?	Yes, I **did.** No, I **didn't.**
Did Mayra **march** in the band? **Did** she **cook** dinner?	Yes, she **did.** No, she **didn't.**
Did all of the students **vote?** **Did** all of them **attend** the assembly?	No, they **didn't.** Yes, they **did.**

I **cheered** for the team last night. I **didn't cheer** for the team yesterday.
Ted **decorated** the gym yesterday. He **didn't decorate** the gym today.
Sonia **danced** at the school dance last night. She **didn't dance** at the school dance last month.
We **marched** in the band yesterday. We **didn't march** in the band on Friday.
They **studied** for their English test last night. They **didn't study** for their science test.

cheer + ed = cheered study + ed = studied stop + ed = stopped

Unit 7

Sonia is a **tall, thin** girl.
She has **long, straight** hair.
She has **big blue** eyes.
She's wearing a **pretty red** sweater.
Mr. Hill is a **short, heavy** man.
He has **curly brown** hair.
He's wearing a **nice black** jacket.

Unit 8

Where **were** you last week?
Where **was** Susan last week?
How long **was** Greg on vacation?
How **was** your vacation?
Where **were** you and Nan yesterday?
Where **were** Fred and Max yesterday?
	I **was** on vacation last week.
	She **was** on vacation too.
	He **was** on vacation for ten days.
	It **was** fun!
	We **were** at the park.
	They **were** at the soccer game.
		How long does it **take** to get to
		    Los Angeles from Chicago?
		It takes about four hours by plane.
		
		How long did it **take** you to get to
		    San Francisco from Los Angeles?
		It took me eight hours by bus.

Were you sick yesterday? **Were** you at school? **Was** Sam at the game last night? **Were** you and Rita at the theater? **Were** Ted and Luis at the gym?	Yes, I **was.** No, I **wasn't.** Yes, he **was.** Yes, we **were.** No, they **weren't.**	was + not = wasn't were + not = weren't

Unit 9

What **are you going to do** tomorrow? What **is** Ted **going to do**? What **is** the weather **going to be** like? Where **are** you and Rita **going to be** tonight? Where **are** Ed and Barb **going to be**?	**I'm going to swim** in the ocean. **He's going to hike** in the mountains. **It's going to rain** tonight. **I'm not going to** go out. **We're going to be** at the dance. **They're going to be** at the dance too.

I'm going to = I am going to He's going to = He is going to We're going to = We are going to	I'm not going to = I am not going to She's not going to = She is not going to She isn't going to = She is not going to

Is Lin **going to play** volleyball tonight? **Is** the weather **going to be** nice tomorrow? **Are** you **going to study** tonight? **Are** your friends **going to be** at the game?	Yes, she **is.** No, it **isn't.** No, **I'm not.** Yes, **they are.**

Unit 10

Could you please give **me** the TV guide? I gave **you** the TV guide.	Could you please give the TV guide to **me**? I gave it to **you.**

Did Ken give **her** the book? No, she gave **him** the book.	Did Ken give the book to **her**? No, she gave it to **him.**

Did Pam and Lucy show **you** the pictures? Yes, they showed **us** the pictures. We showed **them** some pictures, too.	Did Pam and Lucy show the pictures to **you**? Yes, they showed the pictures to **us.** We showed some pictures to **them,** too.

Unit 11

It's fun **to ice skate.** **It's** exciting **to play** hockey. I think **it's** hard **to learn** a new sport.	**Swimming** is fun on a hot day. I like **swimming** in the ocean. Does Greg like downhill **skiing**? No, he thinks **skiing** is dangerous.	Let's **go** to the movies. Let's **have** lunch. Let's **go** ice skating.

Unit 12

Present Progressive	Are you **writing** your newspaper article now?
Simple Past	No, but I **wrote** the first paragraph last night.
Simple Present	But you **work** on the newspaper every Monday, Tuesday, and Wednesday.
Infinitive	I know. But today I want **to work** on my science project.
Future	I'm **going to write** my newspaper article on Thursday.

Is Maria **writing** the sports column now? **Did** it **rain** last night? **Were** you at the dance last night? **Does** Kenji usually go to school dances? **Is** he tall and thin? **Are** Kenji and Alma **going to be** here tomorrow?	Yes, she **is.** No, it **didn't.** No, I **wasn't.** Yes, he **does.** No, he **isn't.** No, they **aren't.**

How **was** your vacation in Florida? When **did** you and your family **go** there? Where **does** Lin usually **go** after school? Why **isn't** Fred **going to be** in class?	It **was** great! We **went** there last week. She usually **goes** home. He's **going to go** to the dentist's office.

INDEX

Numbers indicate units. GS indicates Getting Started.

This page constitutes a continuation of the copyright page.

Illustrations
Julie Anderson (photo collage art) 6TR, 8, 11, 13T, 24, 48B, 53, 104C, 120; Chuck Bracke 95, 105, 106, 115; Rita Daugavietis 17B, 31, 34, 41, 113R, 114; Mike Edsey 97, 99; John Faulkner 7, 10, 17T, 18, 19, 27, 32, 39T, 100, 102T, 117, 118, 123; Dennis Franzen 39B, 44; Tom Garcia 16, 21, 26, 40B, 42, 57, 58, 59, 60, 61, 62, 63T; George Hamblin 38, 76, 79, 82T, 83, 96; Mitch Heinze 107, 111; Tom McKee 29, 30, 37, 67, 68, 69, 70, 71, 72T, 87, 88, 90, 101, 103, 112; Christian Musselman 12, 22B, 33, 43, 53, 63B, 72B, 82B, 92, 102B, 113B, 122; Stephanie O' Shaughnessy 1, 2, 3, 5, 6, 15, 20, 25, 35, 36, 40T, 45, 46, 55, 56, 65, 66, 75, 85, 86; Publishers Services, Inc. 3B, 4, 6B, 8BR, 9, 10T, 11C, 13, 14, 22T, 30B, 31L, 34C, 34B, 54T, 54B, 64, 73, 74, 81, 84, 87, 89, 91, 93, 94, 98, 103C, 114TL, 114B, 116, 117T, 118T, 119, 123, 124; Sandra Scarbeck-Ernst (photo collage art) 50C, 50B, 62T, 71T, 110T, 111T; Mike Sobey 109, 110; Jim Wisniewski 47, 48, 49, 50, 51, 52, 54, 108.

Photographs
Unless otherwise acknowledged, all photographs are the property of ScottForesman. Page abbreviations are as follows: (T) top, (B) bottom, (L) left, (R) right, (C) center. **6:** Superstock; **8CL:** UPI/Bettman; **8CR:** Wide World; **8B:** Wide World; **11:** UPI/Bettman; **48:** Superstock; **53:** Superstock; **62:** Bob Daemmrich/Tony Stone Images; **71:** Jerry Amster/Superstock; **110:** Ben Blankenburg/Stock Boston; **111:** Anestis Diakopoulos/Stock Boston; **114:** Bob Daemmrich/Stock Boston; **116:** USMA; **117:** Steve Webel/Tony Stone Images; **118:** Frank Siteman/Stock Boston; **119T:** The Governor's Office, Arkansas; **120:** Henryk T. Kaiser/Leo deWys, Inc.